THE
FARM
&
CITY
COOKBOOK

KATHRYN MACDONALD
& MARY LOU MORGAN

SECOND STORY
Press

CANADIAN CATALOGUING IN PUBLICATION DATA

MacDonald, Kathryn
The farm & city cookbook

ISBN 0-929005-67-8

1. Cookery. I. Morgan, Mary Lou. II. Title.
III. Title: The farm and city cookbook.

TX714.M3 1994   641.5   C94-932387-X

Illustrations by Farida Zaman
Edited by Susan Lawrence

Printed and bound in Canada

Published by

SECOND STORY PRESS
720 Bathurst Street Suite 301
Toronto, Ontario
M5S 2R4

J.E. MacDonald for sustenance provided.
K.M.

*R.J. Morgan who still doesn't share all his
cooking secrets with me.*
M.L.M.

Contents

Chapter 5   BREADS AND GRAINS 185

Food for Thought — Eating is an Agricultural Act:
How the Food System Works 187

ACKNOWLEDGEMENTS

We thank the women in our communities who contributed recipes and encouraged and supported us while we worked on *The Farm & City Cookbook.*

We celebrate the love of food, cooking skills and confidence that were passed on to us by our foremothers.

We are pleased to be invited to our childrens' homes to share their passion for food and to see their ease in preparing meals for family and friends.

PREFACE

OUR FRIENDSHIP grew out of a meeting in an office tower in downtown Toronto. In August of 1991 we were both appointed to The Ontario Farm Products Marketing Commission, a group of 12 citizens that supervises all the marketing boards in Ontario.

Mary Lou was appointed to bring a consumer point of view and Kathryn to bring a farm woman's perspective to the table, informing discussion and decision making with the knowledge and insights gained through our various experiences.

Mary Lou was part of the start-up and expansion of The Big Carrot, the largest natural food store in Toronto, and of Field to Table, an experimental, nonprofit business that sells affordable nutritious food to low-income city people. Kathryn, on the other hand, is an executive member of the local Ontario Federation of Agriculture and an active member of the Ontario Farm Women's Network, an organization that promotes equality for farm women. Like many farm women, she labours off the farm as well — she worked at *Harrowsmith* magazine during its early years and now acts as an assistant to the local MP while working on her master's degree in public administration at Queen's University.

Perhaps it was our newness and surprise at our appointments that initially drew us together. We quickly found we shared similar philosophies about food, agriculture, the environment and health and women's issues. We also had many of the same concerns and questions about our food system.

Every month after the formal two-day meeting, we would get together and talk until Kathryn's train was ready to board. After we covered personal histories, our families and our love for food, we would muse about life on the farm and life in the city. At first we visited each other's homes but, later on, instead of talking over coffee at the kitchen table, we began using the information highway, faxing from our home computers across the miles.

This book, which grew out of our friendship, combines food for thought and food for the table. The food-for-thought personal stories at the beginning of each chapter reflect our different backgrounds. Mary Lou is firmly rooted in the city, Kathryn's family has been farming for generations. As well, these stories reflect our philosophies about the food system.

When it comes to food for the table, we've chosen recipes that emphasize fresh, wholesome, nutritious ingredients bought in season at your local supermarket or farmers market. Where it's appropriate, we've put the recipes within each chapter in seasonal order, beginning with asparagus and moving through to pumpkin and Christmas recipes. Most of these recipes are easy to prepare because we know that life is busy whether you live in the country or the city. While some may require planning (for example, to soak dried beans the night before), most don't need a great deal of actual time spent in the kitchen.

Kathryn's recipes reflect the traditions of farm cooking, using local in-season foods: recipes like *Rhubarb & Strawberry Crumble*, *Apple Crisp*, and *Corn, Green Pepper & Tomato Salad*. Mary Lou's recipes on the other hand, reflect the rich influence of immigrants on our food: recipes like *Polenta with Meat Sauce*, *Couscous with Vegetables* and *Gobhi Masala*. We've included some meat dishes but, in keeping with the recommendations in Canada's new Food Guide and the growing move to a diet which includes more fresh vegetables and fruits, most of the main dishes emphasize vegetables and grains and most of the desserts emphasize fruits.

We hope this cookbook offers satisfying food for thought as well as for the table. Thank you to all who shared recipes with us.

Bon appetit or *kai orexei*, as the Greeks say.

KATHRYN MACDONALD
Whiteoaks Farm

MARY LOU MORGAN
Toronto

PICNICS & POTLUCKS

THE FARM: YESTERDAY & TODAY

MY CONNECTION WITH FARMING is deep and strong and goes back generations. Today, my husband and I farm in eastern Ontario on land that dips down from a limestone ridge toward a marsh and mud-bottomed lake. It's a beautiful place with spring-fed ponds, cedar snake fences and marsh willow whose stalks turn ox-blood red even before all the snow has melted. Red-winged blackbirds perch on swaying cattails in the marsh and a heron sits atop a slender silver dead sapling among the cattails. Meadows near the marsh are hot and steamy in the summer, because they lie below the breezes that sweep up off the water and over the ridge. And Canada geese return each spring to swim in the swale, eat new seedlings and fight with the cattle over territorial rights for the pasture.

A 1940s photograph, taken from a plane and left for us by the previous owner, shows haystacks near the orchard with the lake in the background. And neighbours say the farm was renowned then for the production of alfalfa seed.

Like the farm of my childhood, this farm supported large families in the past. Milk was shipped to a nearby cheese factory, a few hogs were raised in the piggery and a flock of sheep grazed along the ridge. Livestock chores, haying, gardening (then preserving the harvest from garden and orchard), sewing, mending and community work — these things likely kept the women on this farm busy. However, the land is not richly endowed or generally suited for growing cash crops; we maintain a sustainable balance by grazing livestock and careful husbandry. Caring for the farm requires a lot of work and skill and a full-time commitment by my spouse.

When we moved in, sheep were our first livestock purchase. We bought a small flock of about 25 ewes. Then we drove about the countryside, following ads in weekly newspapers, until we found a suitable ram. Early the following spring, I experienced my first attempts at sheep midwifery. Most of the ewes delivered twin lambs on their own, but some needed assistance. I would try to keep them calm and relaxed while my husband turned a lamb that was breech, or pulled a triplet whose mother was exhausted. On very cold nights, he might come in from the barn with a pair of newborns wrapped in a blanket. We'd lay them near the woodstove where they'd warm up and soon be bouncing around the kitchen. Tucking them back into the blanket for the return trip to the barn was more of a challenge than the trip to the house.

By the time we sold the flock, it had expanded to over 100 ewes. But we had lost the battle with coyotes — small doglike carnivores that grew so brazen they'd come right into the barnyard to find their breakfast. One dawn, I was standing in the bedroom window looking out over the pasture when three coyotes circled a pregnant ewe and took her down. The horrific image of the attackers gnawing at her flesh while she struggled to escape is embedded in my mind forever. My husband and I ran across the yard, but we were too late. We couldn't bear to be responsible for the attacks on our flock, and we couldn't afford the financial loss, either. Shortly afterward, we placed an ad in the paper and sold the flock. Meanwhile, our cattle herd was increasing. We raise primarily Angus cattle — either red or black — and breed the cows to a French Limousin bull. This spring, we added a number of white-faced Hereford heifers (Hereford is a British breed of beef cattle; heifers are young females). The cattle prefer to sleep on the ridge beneath the old apple trees, unless the weather is bad. Then, they crowd against the barn wall to get out of the wind. When it is really bad, they relent and go inside. Every morning, before reaching for my toothbrush, I look out the bathroom window to watch them wake, stand and begin their walk to the feeders.

Our days start at six o'clock and they are long and full. We rent land from neighbours who have moved from the city and don't farm themselves. Their children, waiting for the school bus, wave as I begin the drive to my office in a nearby town where I work for the local member of Parliament. In the winter, the roads can be harrowing and there's no public transit. But in good weather, the drive is a quiet reprieve from a hectic schedule. My route winds along a country road whose population has tripled over the last few years. Ribbons of homes have sprung up in fields and pastures, transforming the landscape. The rough road curves and dips down, over a narrow bridge that spans the Napanee River flowing toward Lake Ontario. I pass through villages that share vibrant histories of water-driven mills and turn-of-the-century factories. Today, they mainly service commuters like myself, passing through.

In the spring, we enthusiastically sow the garden. We plant, dreaming of the harvest, but the limitation of time hampers our good intentions, and in recent years, the garden often succumbs to weeds. It wasn't always this way. Kitchen gardens were extremely important to previous generations of farm families. Mine was no exception.

When I was growing up, a garden separated my family's house and that of my great-aunt Julia and my great-grandmother Lily. Aunt Julia and Grandma Lily were foragers. Grandma had learned these skills from her Wyandot grandmother, and it was my turn to learn. With them, I would journey beyond the garden into the bush on a neighbouring farm, where they gathered hickory nuts and walnuts. As they rummaged around in the grasses beneath huge, spreading trees, I would search for frogs and garter snakes more often than nuts.

My mother's parents lived on a farm, too. Grandma Rose raised turkeys for market. The city of my early childhood was the market — a noisy, chaotic bustle of people. The marketplace was two levels of stalls that opened onto wide sidewalks. In my memories, the building seemed to have no walls. Instead, the vendors tumbled into the streets in a rather haphazard way. And the sunshine reached deep inside.

My grandmother had been going to market for years, and she had a very good stall in a high-traffic area. She would arrange her turkeys on ice to keep them chilled and always sold out before the ice melted. I wanted to walk through the market, peering into other people's stalls, peeking behind their counters to see what treasures lurked beneath the rows of eggs, cheeses, fruits and vegetables. I imagined that I'd be able to piece their lives together by glimpsing the knitting, or picnic basket or coat that was tucked out of sight. But Grandma Rose was a busy no-nonsense woman, who had to get home to check the eggs hatching in the incubator. I suspect I was a bit of a nuisance with my questions and my pestering to be allowed to walk through the market on my own. I seldom got to go with her.

The farm is where I learned about living and dying. It was an extraordinarily rich childhood of imaginary and real adventures, full of life's lessons based on the earth's cycles. I imagine, however, that some statistician in some city office cubicle might have counted my family among the rural poor because we had no money. From one perspective that may be true. But it brings into question the things we value and how we measure ourselves, our families and our communities.

The 100-acre farm of my childhood supported my parents and their seven kids, and it contributed to the support of my great-aunt. My mother sold eggs from the kitchen door, many of her customers coming from Windsor and Detroit. My father sold milk, raised a few calves and grew field crops in the clay loam.

Change, however, is constant, and change came to agriculture in the form of agribusiness. Farmers began to specialize. More and more, my father bought machinery, renting additional land to offset the capital costs, and doing custom work for other farmers. Soon, he was renting and working land along our road and on the next concession. One afternoon in November 1961, he was struck by a car from behind, toppling his tractor and ending his life. My youngest brother had not yet started school. But my mother did not give up the farm for a decade. She hung on with the help of family, neighbours and quiet determination.

Farm women have always worked — in the barns and fields, and in their communities. Like those in my family, women around the world have a long and proud tradition of food production, whether with small family gardens, field crops, animal husbandry or value-added enterprises. Women's involvement with food production continues, only today add off-farm labour to the responsibilities that they shoulder.

K.M.

Picnics, Potlucks & Company Cooking

Say the word "Picnic" and feel the summer heat, hear the breezes rustling in the tree above the picnic table, and imagine the taste of devilled eggs, potato salad and fresh tomato slices in vinegar and basil. Oh, and the desserts: I always hoped to find dark chocolate brownies in the round tin that once held peanut butter.

Every summer on a Sunday in July, my mother's family congregated at a lakeside park. Parents packed baskets of special picnic treats that they knew their children loved. When I was quite young, one aunt and uncle lived near Lake Erie, and they usually brought a bushel of muskmelons with their heady, ripe perfume to family reunions. My father always brought watermelon that he put in a washtub of cold water to chill. As the afternoon progressed, the old men sat in lawn chairs telling stories to each other; the women sat around the cleared table, nursing infants or holding sleepy toddlers; children ran races organized by their fathers and pleaded to be allowed to go into the lake with the teenagers.

Potluck dinners, on the other hand, conjure images of church basements, community halls and neighbours' homes at Christmas. Potlucks are serendipitous. Everyone brings a dish or two and puts it on long tables. Amazingly enough, there is usually a balance between salads, entrées and desserts —

although I can remember hoping that everyone would bring the latter and I'd find the tables laden with tarts, cookies and dessert bars. But it never did happen.

Country cooks became known across their communities for particular dishes and could be counted on to bring the best baked beans in the county, or the creamiest potato salad, irresistible coleslaw, or a melt-in-your-mouth apple pie, fragrant with cinnamon and nutmeg. These are the same women who prepare food for fundraisers. Every fall hand-painted signs spring up in rural villages advertising the church supper and the women's institute fête.

Neighbours on our road host a holiday potluck each year. Once the tree has been decorated, we gather as neighbours have likely done for generations, to share food and friendship mid-winter. We wrap hot baking dishes in towels to keep them warm as we transport them through the snow.

I remember early one spring, six friends got together at our house to have a wild potluck, each bringing something harvested from nature. We feasted on dandelion salad with winter onions that grew in the fencerow, fiddleheads, beaver (a gift from the local trapper), wild rice and a dessert sweetened with maple syrup. While the food was memorable, it is the conversation and laughter that I warmly recall.

It is the camaraderie of picnics and potlucks that makes them truly special. The food always tastes better than it does at the kitchen table. The conversation is always livelier. Picnics and potlucks embrace the entire family, a group of friends or the whole community. Picnics and potlucks may be simple or elaborate. What they require is people to share portable food, a carrying container or two and a sense of adventure. Enjoy.

K.M.

Corn, Green Pepper & Tomato Salad

This colourful dish grew out of my overexuberance at a neighbour's farmgate vegetable stand when I purchased more corn than we could eat for dinner. I combined the leftover corn with other seasonal vegetables to produce this flavourful summer salad.

¼ *cup* olive oil *50 mL*
¼ *cup* dry white wine *50 mL*
2 *Tbsp* lemon juice *25 mL*
2 cloves garlic, chopped
salt and pepper
3 *cups* corn *750 mL*
½ green pepper, chopped
1 small red onion, thinly sliced
1 tomato, diced
2 *Tbsp* chopped parsley *25 mL*
2 *tsp* chopped basil leaves *10 mL*

Heat oil over medium heat and add wine, lemon juice, garlic and a sprinkle of salt and pepper. Simmer for 5 minutes.

Add corn, and cook for 3 minutes. Remove from heat. Add remaining ingredients. Toss. Serve at room temperature.

Makes 6 servings.

▼ ▼ ▼ ▼ ▼ ▼ ▼ ▼ ▼ ▼ ▼ ▼ ▼ ▼ ▼

CORN

Corn is a Canadian staple. Often called
Mother Earth, it is a divine symbol of
woman, and is celebrated by native people as
a gift from the Great Spirit. The golden
grains are also called *maïs* or *maize*. Dried
kernels were often stored underground in
mounds, in case of a shortage of food in winter when it could be made into a potage or
ground into flour. Originating in Central
America, corn was traded northward and was
well established in North America by the
time the first Europeans arrived.

▲ ▲ ▲ ▲ ▲ ▲ ▲ ▲ ▲ ▲ ▲ ▲ ▲ ▲ ▲ ▲

▼ ▼ ▼ ▼ ▼ ▼ ▼ ▼ ▼ ▼ ▼ ▼ ▼ ▼ ▼

VINEGAR

When bacteria develops in fermented fruit
juice (or wine), vinegar results. In fact, the
French *vin aigre* translates into sour wine.
Vinegar is a mild acetic acid, which is thought
to aid disgestion by breaking down fibrous
vegetables. While vinegars are made from
various fruits or wines, cider vinegar is made
from apples. The best cider vinegar is made
from whole apples, ground, then cold-
pressed, fermented naturally in wooden casks
and aged. Lesser ciders are made with
crushed peelings and cores and are artificially
rushed through the process.

▲ ▲ ▲ ▲ ▲ ▲ ▲ ▲ ▲ ▲ ▲ ▲ ▲ ▲ ▲ ▲

Rice & Corn
with Cider Dressing

If you are not taking this salad to a picnic or potluck, it keeps well in the fridge for a few days, making a meal later in the week very quick, indeed.

4 cups cooked rice *1 L*
2 cups cooked corn *500 mL*
½ green pepper, chopped
6 green onions, chopped
½ *cup* vegetable oil *125 mL*
½ *cup* cider vinegar *125 mL*
2 *Tbsp* sugar *25 mL*
1 *tsp* celery seed *5 mL*
½ *tsp* dry mustard *1 mL*
½ *tsp* salt *2 mL*
dash pepper

Mix together rice, corn, green pepper and onions.

In a saucepan, bring remaining ingredients to the boiling point.

Pour over rice mixture. Marinate in the fridge a few hours. Bring to room temperature for serving.

Makes 8 to 10 servings.

GLENDA'S RICE SALAD

*This recipe was brought to an office potluck luncheon,
where it was an enormous hit. Busy cooks like it too —
serve half now and store half in the fridge
to serve 4 or 5 days later.*

2 *cups* cooked rice *500 mL*
1½ *cups* chopped onions *375 mL*
1 *cup* chopped celery *250 mL*
1 *cup* fresh or frozen peas, blanched *250 mL*
1 *cup* chopped green pepper *250 mL*
½ *cup* vegetable oil *125 mL*
3 *Tbsp* soya sauce *45 mL*
2 *tsp* curry powder *10 mL*
1 *tsp* salt *5 mL*
½ *tsp* sugar *2 mL*

Mix rice and vegetables together in bowl.

Heat remaining ingredients in saucepan until they come
to a boil; pour over rice mixture.

Cool. Refrigerate at least 2 hours (although best left to
marinate overnight).

Makes 8 servings.

SUMMER LENTIL SALAD

Lentils in soup are a winter staple at our house, but traditionally, they haven't been part of our summer diet. A few years ago, I visited Victoria, where I stayed with a long-distance colleague who served a lentil salad. Since then, I've been experimenting to find the right combination of herbs, fruits and vegetables. Summer Lentil Salad *is the delicious result.*

4 cups water *1 L*
1 cup brown lentils *250 mL*
1 clove garlic
1 bay leaf
½ tsp ground cumin *2 mL*
salt and pepper
1 orange, peeled and seeded
1 lemon
1 lime
1 cucumber, peeled and seeded
¼ red onion, thinly sliced
2 large tomatoes, peeled and chopped
2 Tbsp chopped fresh mint *25 mL*
¼ cup chopped fresh parsley *50 mL*
2 Tbsp olive oil *25 mL*
2 tsp balsamic vinegar *10 mL*

Bring water to boil in pot. Add lentils, garlic, bay leaf, cumin, salt and pepper.

Reduce heat, cover and cook until lentils are tender, about 30 minutes.

Meanwhile, remove pith (white part) from orange sections; chop orange into large bowl.

Squeeze juice from lemon and lime and stir into chopped orange.

Cut cucumber into quarters lengthwise; slice thinly and add to bowl. Stir in onion slices, chopped tomatoes, mint and parsley.

When lentils are cooked, remove bay leaf and garlic clove. Drain lentils in sieve. Chill under cold running water.

Stir lentils into bowl. Stir in oil and vinegar. Add salt and pepper to taste and toss gently.

Makes 4 servings.

▼ ▼ ▼ ▼ ▼ ▼ ▼ ▼ ▼ ▼ ▼ ▼ ▼ ▼ ▼

EGGS

Eggs provide almost a perfect source of
protein because of their amino acid pattern.
Depending on the hens' diet, eggs may also
be a good vitamin and mineral source,
although concentration varies. Yolks that are
deep yellow to orange in colour, for example,
are high in vitamin A. Eggs should be stored
in the fridge; however, before using them in
recipes, eggs should be allowed to return
to room temperature.

DEVILLED EGGS

These eggs are a staple for picnics and summer buffets,
but be careful to keep them well chilled.

6 hard-boiled eggs
¼ cup minced fresh mushrooms *50 mL*
1 Tbsp mayonnaise *15 mL*
1 tsp Dijon mustard *5 mL*
salt, black pepper and cayenne pepper
minced parsley, chives or tarragon
sweet paprika

Halve eggs lengthwise. Remove yolks and mash in bowl with remaining ingredients.

Stuff mixture into egg whites and sprinkle with sweet paprika.

To carry to picnic or potluck, pack tightly in container in upright position.

Makes 12 servings.

BLENDER MAYONNAISE

*This mayonnaise can be made with herb or cider vinegar,
olive or vegetable oil — or a mixture of each. Depending
on what I'm making, I stir in a generous spoonful of
mustard, one or two chopped garlic cloves or
fresh chopped herbs in season.*

1 cup vegetable oil *250 mL*
1 egg
1 Tbsp vinegar *15 mL*
½ tsp dry mustard *2 mL*
¼ tsp salt *1 mL*

Have oil ready beside blender. Put egg in the blender;
add vinegar, salt, and dried mustard. Blend at full speed for
30 seconds.

In a steady stream, *slowly* add oil. (Halfway through,
you'll hear a sort of plop, as the mayonnaise sets.) Turn off
the machine. There will be a little oil on top; stir it in.

Pour mayonnaise into a jar, cover and keep refrigerated.
(On rare occasions, the mayonnaise curdles or does not set.
Transfer everything into a bowl, put another egg into the
blender, and at highest speed, slowly pour in the mistake. It
will take this time!)

Keeps in refrigerator for up to 1 week.

Makes 1 cup (250 mL).

PICKLED MUSHROOMS

*Once I was fortunate enough to live near a mushroom
farm. Occasionally, we had more mushrooms than could
be eaten fresh, and experimentation led to this recipe that
could be stored in the fridge for weeks,
pending a picnic or potluck.*

2 lb fresh mushrooms *1 kg*

1 large sweet green pepper, cut into
narrow 1 inch (2.5 cm) strips

1 stalk celery, cut thinly crosswise

1½ cups white vinegar *375 mL*

1½ cups water *375 mL*

1 Tbsp pickling spice *15 mL*

½ cup olive oil *125 mL*

½ cup vegetable oil *125 mL*

¼ cup lemon juice *50 mL*

1 clove garlic, quartered

½ tsp paprika *2 mL*

¼ tsp dry mustard *1 mL*

½ tsp Worcestershire sauce *2 mL*

½ tsp salt *2 mL*

Bring all of the ingredients to a boil, and boil gently for 5
minutes. Spoon the mushrooms, pepper strips and celery into
jars. Cover with the marinade. Refrigerate at least 24 hours
before serving.

Makes 8 cups (2 L).

OLD-FASHIONED MACARONI SALAD

This traditional salad can just as easily be made with potatoes. Substitute 8 cups of cooked, cubed potatoes for the macaroni. Depending on the season, you may wish to add blanched peas, string beans or tomato wedges. If you omit the bacon, you can add cubes of cooked ham and Cheddar cheese.

3 cups macaroni, cooked and rinsed *750 mL*
4 hard-boiled eggs, chopped
½ cup quartered fresh mushrooms *125 mL*
3 green onions, chopped
4 radishes, sliced thinly
1 stalk celery, sliced thinly
1 cucumber, halved and sliced
½ sweet green pepper, slivered
½ sweet red pepper, slivered
¼ cup chopped chives, parsley or dill *50 mL*
3 Tbsp chopped capers *45 mL*
1 cup mayonnaise *250 mL*
1 clove garlic, minced
1 Tbsp Dijon mustard *15 mL*
5 strips bacon (optional)
½ Tbsp sesame seeds, toasted (optional) *7 mL*

Cook macaroni in boiling water in large pot for 15 minutes or until al dente. Rinse.

Stir all ingredients except sesame seeds together, adding enough mayonnaise to moisten pasta.

Keep chilled until serving time. Sprinkle with sesame seeds.

Makes 8 servings.

▼ ▼ ▼ ▼ ▼ ▼ ▼ ▼ ▼ ▼ ▼ ▼ ▼ ▼ ▼

MUSHROOMS

Since most of the flavour of mushrooms is in the skin, it's best to wipe them with a cloth rather than wash them. If you must wash, handle carefully. The stems are not as tender as the caps. For this recipe you may wish to reserve the stems for soup stock. Although they're grown in the dark, mushrooms are high in vitamin D and have other nutrients such as phosphorus and iron — and almost no calories. To keep raw mushrooms white on a vegetable tray, sprinkle them with lemon juice.

▲ ▲ ▲ ▲ ▲ ▲ ▲ ▲ ▲ ▲ ▲ ▲ ▲ ▲ ▲ ▲

JERK CHICKEN

Jerk is both a particular Jamaican seasoning and a cooking technique. Special seasonings are rubbed into meat, which is marinated before being cooked slowly over medium heat. Delsie Hyatt, who works at Field to Table, has taught all of us to make this recipe but we still swear Delsie, who's from Jamaica, makes it best. When potlucks are held at her children's school, the teachers phone and beg her to bring this chicken.

3 *lb* chicken legs *1.5 kg*
1 onion, diced
2 cloves garlic, minced
½ sweet green pepper, diced
1 *tsp* dried thyme or 3 sprigs fresh thyme *5 mL*
pinch allspice
2 *Tbsp* soya sauce *25 mL*
2 *Tbsp* jerk sauce *25 mL*

Remove fat and skin from chicken legs separate at the bone. Wash the meat in water with 2 Tbsp (25 mL) of vinegar added to it to cut grease. Using a wooden spoon combine remaining ingredients in bowl and rub into chicken. Marinate in the refrigerator several hours or overnight. Preheat oven to 350°F (180°C). Cover the chicken and bake for 1 hour, turning once. Remove lid and cook for 15 more minutes. Serve with *Rice & Peas*.

Makes 6 servings.

HOMEMADE JERK
SEASONING

If you live in the country and can't buy prepared jerk sauce, this is a from-scratch recipe that keeps up to three months in the refrigerator The flavours need several hours to meld. Scotch bonnet peppers are best but habanero or other hot peppers can be substituted. Avoid touching your eyes when working with these hot peppers and wash hands thoroughly afterward.

1 Tbsp black peppercorns *15 mL*
1 Tbsp whole corriander seeds *15 mL*
½ Tbsp all spice berries *7 mL*
½ Tbsp salt *7 mL*
1 tsp nutmeg *5 mL*
1 tsp ground cinnamon *5 mL*
10 green onions, chopped
1" gingerroot peeled *2.5 cm*
4 cloves garlic
2 Tbsp soya sauce *25 mL*
2 Tbsp vinegar *25 mL*
2 hot peppers
¼ cup fresh thyme *50 mL*

Grind peppercorns, whole corriander, allspice berries, nutmeg, cinnamon and salt in spice grinder.

In a food processor pulse spices, onions, gingerroot, garlic, soya sauce and vinegar.

Then add peppers and thyme, so that mixture has a rough texture.

Makes ¾ cup (175 mL).

RICE & PEAS

Rice and peas go with Jerk Chicken *like steak goes with frites. Pigeon peas for this recipe can be purchased dried, frozen or occasionally fresh in a Jamaican store but red kidney beans can be substituted. When Delsie visits family in Jamaica, she takes rice, cooking oil, flour and sugar. Food prices for basic staples are astronomical there because most food is imported, but fresh mangoes and jelly coconuts can be picked in the backyard.*

3 cups water *750 mL*
2 cups long-grain rice *500 mL*
½ cup red kidney beans, cooked *125 mL*
½ tsp dried thyme or *1* sprig fresh *2 mL*
1 cup coconut milk *250 mL*
1 bay leaf
1 onion, diced
2 cloves garlic, minced
1 stick cinnamon
salt and pepper

Bring water to boil in a large pot. Add all ingredients.
Cover and simmer gently for 25 to 30 minutes.
Remove bay leaf and serve.

Makes 6 to 8 servings.

MAKE-YOUR-OWN COCONUT MILK

Fresh coconut milk is not the milk inside the coconut but the flesh of the fruit, which has been grated and squeezed. If you have the patience you can also open a fresh coconut, pry out the pieces, grate the meat and blend it with 1¼ cups (300 mL) of water. Freeze any leftover milk for future use.

2 *cups* shredded unsweetended coconut 500 mL
2 *cups* water 500 mL

Put coconut into blender. Add water, blend for a few minutes and strain through fine sieve.

Makes 2½ cups (625 mL).

COLD CHICKEN LOAF

*For picnics, cold buffets and summer potluck suppers, you
can't beat this loaf. It's easy to prepare, slices beautifully,
tastes delicious and travels well.*

4 *lb* ground chicken *2 kg*
2 onions, halved
2 stalks celery
10 peppercorns
1 carrot
¼ *cup* chopped parsley *50 mL*
2 *tsp* salt *10 mL*
2 *cups* bread crumbs (4 slices bread) *500 mL*
1 *cup* milk *250 mL*
2 large eggs
½ *cup* finely chopped onion *125 mL*
1 *tsp* salt *5 mL*
¼ *tsp* pepper *1 mL*
½ *cup* chicken stock *125 mL*

Cover the chicken with water in a large stockpot or
Dutch oven; add onions, celery, peppercorns, carrot, parsley
and salt. Gently boil until the chicken is tender.

Strain and reserve ½ cup (125 mL) stock for loaf (reserve
the remaining stock for soup; freeze until a later date).

In large bowl, mix bread crumbs, milk, eggs, chopped
onion, salt and pepper.

Stir in ground chicken and ½ cup (125 mL) stock; mix well.

Line the bottom of a loaf pan (4½" x 8½" x 2¾"/1.5 L) with waxed paper. Butter paper and sides of pan. Press mixture down well; smooth top. Cover with foil.

Set in a larger pan in 1 inch (2.5 cm) of water; poach for 1 hour in 375°F (190°C) oven.

Remove foil and continue poaching for another 10 minutes.

Cool and chill thoroughly before turning out onto platter.

Makes 16 servings.

▼ ▼ ▼ ▼ ▼ ▼ ▼ ▼ ▼ ▼ ▼ ▼ ▼ ▼ ▼

BEEF/LAMB

Beef provides all eight of the amino acids we require and is also a good source of vitamins A and B, and a form of iron that is easily absorbed by the body. Beef may be quickly sautéed along with vegetables in a stir-fry, mixed with other ground meats to make sauces for pasta or the filling of a tourtière, or it may be marinated, roasted and chilled as in *Orange Marinated Beef*. Modest portions of meat in the diet — three or four times a week — are a healthy source of necessary nutrients. Lamb curries are popular in some cultures, leg of lamb with mint sauce in others, lamb broiled with wine and Dijon mustard sauce in still others. Like other red meats, lamb is a source of protein, iron and the B vitamins (thiamin, riboflavin and niacin).

▲ ▲ ▲ ▲ ▲ ▲ ▲ ▲ ▲ ▲ ▲ ▲ ▲ ▲ ▲

ORANGE MARINATED BEEF

*This is an easy recipe to prepare – it does, however,
require planning. The meat is marinated for 48 hours,
turned periodically and popped into the oven. It's great
with potato salad and other traditional
picnic accoutrements.*

4 lb boneless roast (bottom round or rump) *2 kg*
1 Tbsp pickling spice *15 mL*
12 peppercorns
1 bay leaf
2 cups orange juice *500 mL*
½ cup red wine vinegar *125 mL*
2 small onions, chopped

Pierce roast all over with fork. Put pickling spice, peppercorns and bay leaf into tea caddy or muslin bag; put this into
a pot with juice, vinegar and onions. Heat to the boil, and
simmer 5 minutes. Cool the marinade.

Remove the spice bag. Set roast in large glass or pottery
bowl; pour marinade over roast. Cover and refrigerate, turning frequently, for 48 hours.

Put marinade and meat in roasting pan. Roast at 350°F
(180°C) for about 2½ hours. Cool and slice as thinly as possible. Arrange slices on platter for buffet or potluck, or in a
carrier for a picnic.

Makes 8 to 10 servings.

LAMB LOAF

*This loaf slices well when cold. It tastes great on rye bread
with alfalfa sprouts and Dijon mustard.*

2 slices bacon
1 lb ground lamb *500 g*
¼ sweet green pepper, diced
1 small onion, diced
1 tomato, peeled and diced (or ½ cup/125 mL canned)
½ cup rolled oats *125 mL*
¼ tsp salt *1 mL*
¼ tsp savory *1 mL*
¼ tsp cinnamon *1 mL*
dash pepper
dash celery seed
dash cloves

Cook bacon in skillet for 10 minutes or until browned;
crumble.

In mixing bowl, stir all ingredients together.

Press into loaf pan (8" x 4"/1.5 L) and bake at 350°F
(180°C) for 45 to 60 minutes.

Cool slightly before removing from pan.

Makes 4 servings.

▼

SPANAKOPITA

*Georgia Nayyar, who contributed this recipe, was born in
Greece but became a superb cook of East Indian dishes
after she married an East Indian. This special recipe
celebrates her Greek heritage. Phyllo dough is available
frozen in most supermarkets. It needs to be defrosted in
the refrigerator. When completely defrosted, unwrap the
dough, unroll it and cover immediately with a damp tea
towel to prevent it from drying out.
Take out a sheet at a time.*

3 Tbsp butter *45 mL*
10 green onions or 1 large onion, chopped
4 cloves garlic, chopped
1 package spinach, washed and chopped
2 Tbsp dried dill (optional) *25 mL*
2 Tbsp chopped fresh parsley *25 mL*
½ cup grated feta cheese *125 mL*
4 large eggs
salt and pepper
¾ cup melted butter *175 mL*
1 package phyllo dough

Melt 3 Tbsp (45 mL) butter in skillet; sauté onions and
garlic until soft but not brown. Mix in spinach, dill and parsley. Cook over medium heat 5 minutes. Remove from heat
and drain off any liquid in pan. Stir in cheese, eggs, salt and
pepper.

Brush a shallow pan or baking sheet with some of the melted butter.

Remove 1 phyllo sheet from under tea towel. Lay on pan and brush with butter. Repeat, stacking phyllo sheets until half of them have been used. Spread filling evenly over surface of stacked phyllo sheets.

Preheat oven to 375°F (190°C).

You are now ready to make the top crust. Stack phyllo sheets on top of filling, one by one, brushing each one with butter. Fold over the edges about 2 inches (5 cm) on each side. Brush the top with remaining butter. Sprinkle with a few drops of water to prevent pastry from curling.

Bake about 45 minutes until top is golden brown. Cut into squares not smaller than 2 inches (5 cm).

Makes 6 servings.

THREE-PIE PASTRY

*One of Dad's sisters shared this recipe with me. It makes
a fine flaky pastry that is delicious with a tourtière or an
apple pie. It's a great time saver because it can be formed
into balls and stored in the refrigerator or
freezer for another day.*

4½ *cups* flour *1.125 mL*
1 tsp salt *5 mL*
¼ *tsp* baking soda *1 mL*
1 lb lard *500 g*
1 Tbsp vinegar *15 mL*
1 egg, beaten

Combine flour, salt, baking soda and lard in large bowl.

Cut in lard, using pastry cutter, until mixture is the size
of small peas.

Add enough cold water to vinegar to make 1 cup (250 mL);
stir in egg.

Add to flour mixture, stirring with fork until mixture
forms ball. Roll into 3 balls. Chill in refrigerator before
rolling out on floured surface.

Makes enough for 3 double-crust pies.

TOURTIÈRE

*For many years a New Year's tradition, tourtière is also a
good dish to take to a potluck supper. You can freeze
extra pies for up to three months.*

2 *lb* lean ground pork *1 kg*
2 *lb* lean ground beef *1 kg*
1 large onion, finely chopped
¼ *tsp* sage *1 mL*
¼ *tsp* pepper *1 mL*
1½ *tsp* salt *7 mL*
2 *cups* mashed potatoes *500 mL*
pastry for 3 double-crust pies

Brown meat, onion and spices in large skillet or Dutch
oven over medium heat until brown but not dry.

Stir in mashed potatoes.

Line 3 pie plates with pastry, and fill with meat mixture;
top with pastry; slash so steam can escape.

Bake at 350°F (180°C) for 45 to 60 minutes until crust is
golden brown.

Makes 3 pies.

HOME-BAKED BEANS

*Nutritious, flavourful and satisfying, baked beans are a
favourite in the country. It's hard to imagine a potluck
supper without them. When I first started keeping house,
a friend shared this recipe which was her mother's. It's
become a favourite of my friends and family. Although it
takes a long time to cook, it requires very little
time in the kitchen.*

2 cups navy beans *500 mL*
1 small onion, minced
1½ tsp salt *7 mL*
4 Tbsp molasses *60 mL*
4 Tbsp tomato ketchup or paste *60 mL*
1 tsp dry mustard *5 mL*
¼ lb salt pork or 4 slices bacon *125 g*

Put beans, onion and salt in large cooking kettle and
cover with water.

Cover and simmer until the skin on the beans bursts,
about 2 hours.

Drain; save the liquid.

Mix molasses, ketchup and mustard into 1 cup (250 mL)
of the reserved liquid.

Put half of the pork in the bottom of large bean pot; add
beans; top with remaining pork.

Pour molasses mixture over beans. Add more of the reserved liquid to cover beans.

Cover and bake slowly at 300°F (150°C) for 4½ hours; uncover and continue baking for another half hour.

Makes 8 servings

▼ ▼ ▼ ▼ ▼ ▼ ▼ ▼ ▼ ▼ ▼ ▼ ▼ ▼ ▼

BEANS

Like corn and tomatoes, navy beans are native to the Americas. Beans, nuts, whole grains and other legumes offer incomplete protein — eggs, milk, meat and fish have the most complete protein of all foods. To make a dish that offers a complete protein, cheese is often added to pasta, and pork is often combined with beans. Soaking beans in a glass bowl in ample water overnight shortens the cooking time generally by half. You will need a large bowl (avoid metal), and add at least three times as much water as volume of dried beans — dried beans swell to double their size. However, old beans may not become tender regardless of cooking time. As a rule, 1 cup of dried beans yields 3 cups of cooked.

▲ ▲ ▲ ▲ ▲ ▲ ▲ ▲ ▲ ▲ ▲ ▲ ▲ ▲ ▲

GNOCCHI

*My mother-in-law, Armida Morgan, is the best cook I
know. Coming from the Venetian part of Italy as a child,
she cooks in the northern Italian style, but is constantly
experimenting and trying new recipes. She uses inexpensive ingredients, carefully chosen herbs, long slow cooking
to meld flavours and much love and care. By example, she
has passed down her love of food to her children and
grandchildren. We still call her long distance for advice
halfway through a recipe when we need to be reminded of
the exact combination of ingredients. This recipe, a modi-
fication of the traditional potato gnocchi, can be served
with either of the following tomato-based sauces.*

1 lb ricotta cheese, drained *475 g*
1 egg
2 cups unbleached flour *500 mL*
dash nutmeg

Mix cheese and egg together in bowl.

Add flour and nutmeg and mix gently with your hands
until it begins to hold together.

Divide dough into 6 pieces. Take each piece and roll out
into a rope about the thickness of your thumb on a floured
board. Cut the dough into little pillows the size of your
thumb.

Roll on back of tines of fork to make indentations to hold
sauce.

Place on a baking sheet, layering with waxed paper and put in freezer for 15 minutes or several hours until ready to cook. This keeps their shape and prevents them from getting sticky.

Bring large pot of salted water to boil.

Drop in ¼ of gnocchi at a time and cook about 2 to 3 minutes until they rise to the surface.

Remove with a slotted spoon and place in serving bowl with a little tomato sauce to keep them from sticking together.

Put bowl in a warm oven and add to it as the gnocchi are ready. Add more sauce just before serving.

Makes 6 servings.

Two-Meats Tomato Sauce

This sauce works well with gnocchi and pasta. The mixture of beef, pork and spices gives a unique taste. It's so popular in our house that I usually double the recipe.

1 Tbsp butter *15 mL*
1 Tbsp olive oil *15 mL*
1 onion, diced
2 cloves garlic, minced
¾ lb lean ground beef *375 g*
¼ lb lean ground pork *125 g*
pinch nutmeg
¼ tsp cinnamon *1 mL*
1 tsp dried rosemary *5 mL*
½ tsp dried basil *2 mL*
salt and pepper
4 cups Italian plum tomatoes *1 L*
1 cup water *250 mL*

Melt butter and olive oil in skillet. Sauté onion and garlic until softened. Add meat and cook until no longer pink, about 5 minutes. Stir in herbs and spices. Stir in tomatoes, 1 cup (250 mL) of water; simmer gently, uncovered, until thick, about 1 hour.

Makes 4 cups (1 L), enough for 1 lb (500 g) pasta or gnocchi.

VEGETARIAN TOMATO SAUCE

This is a very quick and simple sauce. Fresh tomatoes can be used in season. Roma or Italian plum tomatoes, which have little water and few seeds, cook into a nice thick sauce.

¼ cup olive oil *50 mL*
1 onion, chopped
4 cups chopped Italian plum tomatoes *1 L*
salt and pepper
fresh basil leaves

Heat olive oil in pot.

Sauté onion over medium heat until soft.

Add tomatoes and cook gently until sauce thickens, about 25 minutes.

Add salt and pepper to taste and several fresh basil leaves.

Makes 3 cups (750 mL), enough for ¾ lb (750 g) pasta or gnocchi.

NICHOLAS'S BLACK BEAN SOUP

Homemade soup is a real treat and ideal for company because it can be made ahead and served with a salad with little fuss. Some time is needed for preparation – you must soak the beans overnight – but the results are well worthwhile. My son is an excellent cook although we tease him that he uses garlic in everything. He's a confirmed meat-eater but his partner, sister and friends are vegetarians and he has had to adapt his recipes to suit them.

2 cups dried black beans *500 mL*
½ cup olive oil *125 mL*
3 cups diced onions *750 mL*
12 cloves garlic, chopped
3 Tbsp ground cumin *45 mL*
2 Tbsp oregano *25 mL*
3 bay leaves
1 tsp salt *5 mL*
1 tsp black pepper *5 mL*
12 cups water *3 L*
2 small sweet red peppers, diced
⅓ cup minced parsley *75 mL*
2 Tbsp lemon juice *25 mL*
⅓ cup sour cream or yogurt *75 mL*

Soak beans overnight. Drain and rinse.

Heat olive oil in soup pot and sauté onions and garlic until softened.

Add cumin, oregano, bay leaves, salt and pepper, stirring until oil coats spices.

Stir in black beans and water. Cook, covered, on low heat 2 hours until beans are very soft.

Purée half the soup in a blender or food processor. Return to stove.

Cook another 30 minutes.

Stir in red peppers, parsley and lemon juice.

Cook another 10 minutes.

Remove bay leaves. Just before serving, stir in sour cream or yogurt.

Makes 10 servings.

WHITE BEAN SOUP WITH PINE NUT PESTO

Beans are a rich source of vegetable protein, complex car-bohydrates and water-soluble dietary fibre. As well, they're high in B vitamins and minerals. Most tradition-al dishes — tortillas and beans, baked beans with bread, and rice and lentils — combine beans with grain or cereal protein. These simple combinations, used for centuries, provide all the essential protein needed.

2 cups dried white kidney beans *500 mL*
12 cups water *3 L*
pinch saffron (optional)
2 carrots, diced
2 potatoes, cubed
2 leeks, chopped
1 cup chopped onions *250 mL*
2 cups chopped tomatoes *500 mL*
2 bay leaves

PINE NUT PESTO
3 Tbsp olive oil *45 mL*
3 Tbsp pine nuts *45 mL*
2 Tbsp tomato paste *25 mL*
4 cloves garlic

Soak beans overnight. Drain and rinse.

Cook beans and water in large pot, covered, for 1 hour.

Stir in saffron and remaining ingredients.

Cook until beans are very soft, at least another hour. Remove bay leaves.

For PINE NUT PESTO, blend all ingredients in a blender or food processor.

Stir PINE NUT PESTO into soup 30 minutes before serving.

Makes 6 to 8 servings.

CHINESE HOT POT

This is the perfect lingering meal for a blustery winter evening when you have friends over. Place a hot pot or fondue pot with its own heat source in the centre of the table and fill it with either a vegetarian or chicken stock. Guests choose from a beautifully displayed platter of bite-sized ingredients, cook their own meal and transfer it to their bowl. At the end, serve rice with the thickened broth poured over it. Chopsticks are the best utensils for this meal.

8 cups stock *2 L*
2 tsp rice wine or sherry (optional) *10 mL*
2 tsp soya sauce or tamari *10 mL*
2 blocks tofu, cubed
½ Chinese cabbage, cut in wedges
2 cups fresh bean sprouts *500 mL*
1 bunch green onions, cut in 4 inch (10 cm) pieces
6 shiitake mushrooms, presoaked if dried
8 oz cellophane noodles, presoaked *250 g*
1 cup snow peas, trimmed *250 mL*
1 small bok choy, shredded
1 carrot, thinly sliced
¼ package spinach
1 lb shrimp (shells on) *500 g*
2 boneless chicken breasts, cubed

Cut and prepare ingredients beforehand and refrigerate. Use the different colours and shapes to create an interesting display.

Heat stock, wine and soya sauce in a pot on the stove and pour into a fondue pot.

Offer tamari or soya sauce and hot Chinese chili sauce in small bowls on the table.

Makes 6 servings.

POLENTA WITH MEAT SAUCE

Polenta, a thick corn porridge often served with a rich meat sauce, is a traditional Venetian dish. This recipe was originally made with stewing meat but pork tenderloin turns it into a company meal.

2 Tbsp olive oil *25 mL*
2 Tbsp butter *25 mL*
1 small onion, diced
1 carrot, diced
1 stalk celery, diced
½ cup chopped fresh parsley *125 mL*
2 cloves garlic, minced
2 pork tenderloins
4 cups Italian plum tomatoes *1 L*
½ cup white wine *125 mL*
2 bay leaves
pinch nutmeg, rosemary, sage and thyme

Heat oil and butter in skillet over medium-high heat. Sauté onion, carrot, celery, parsley and garlic for 5 to 8 minutes or until carrot is soft. Meanwhile, slice tenderloins into 1-inch (2.5 cm) thick slices. Brown tenderloin slices in skillet until no longer pink, about 5 minutes. Stir in tomatoes, wine, bay leaves, nutmeg, rosemary, sage and thyme; simmer for 45 minutes while you make polenta. Remove bay leaves before serving.

Makes 4 servings

POLENTA

This recipe makes enough for two meals and is delicious reheated the next day in the microwave or skillet or grilled. For a richly satisfying variation, add chick peas or kidney beans at the last minute, slice each piece of polenta in half like a sandwich, insert a slice of blue cheese, then top with meat sauce.

8 cups water *2 L*
1 Tbsp salt *15 mL*
2½ cups yellow cornmeal *625 mL*

Bring water and salt to boil in large deep pot. Gradually pour in cornmeal, stirring constantly with long wooden spoon. Cook over low heat, stirring occasionally, for about 35 minutes. Gradually bubbles will get larger and cornmeal on bottom of pot will begin to form crust. When polenta is thick enough to hold its shape, turn out onto wooden board to form a cake about 3 inches (7.5 cm) thick. Cut into squares using a piece of thread. Top with meat sauce.

Makes 8 servings

GARDEN
FARE

THE CITY STORY: BUYING FOR COMMUNITY

IN THE HEART OF TORONTO'S trendy Queen Street West district, across the street from the continuous live action of City TV's Speaker's Corner, is the Queen Street Market, a lively collection of food boutiques. Here, carrot juice, brown rice with gomasio, pizza slices, poutine from Wild Bill's BBQ, Chinese lemongrass chicken, German meat loaf and sauerkraut sandwiches compete for everyone's attention and lunch money. A produce store and wine stall complete the cast in this renovated chicken slaughterhouse, which sold freshly killed kosher chicken to discriminating customers from 1914 until it closed in 1985. In 1837, the property was donated to the city for the establishment of a food market to serve residents on the west side of Toronto, so the market has come full circle.

If you go back outside, past the teenage panhandlers, down the interlocking brick walkway, to the stairs in the rear you'll find the bright high-ceilinged offices of FoodShare, an umbrella organization dedicated to ending hunger and improving access to affordable nutritious foods. Programs for community gardens, baby and school nutrition, community kitchens and a hunger hotline staffed by volunteers are all housed here.

I am the manager of one of FoodShare's projects, called Field to Table. Field to Table was sparked when two farmers and an inner city community worker, sharing ideas over some beer, puzzled over the fact that although there is lots of food in Canada (in fact acres of food are plowed under every year for lack of a market), urban hunger is constantly in the news. The farmers thought it might be a good idea to load up a semi trailer of second-grade produce and pull into an inner city parking lot to sell directly to the public. In 1992, a community development worker and I came up with an innovative business plan to link farmers and inner city people to challenge hunger and poverty and christened it Field to Table.

I was hired because of my business background in the retail food sector, at The Big Carrot, a large natural food supermarket in Toronto. As president, manager and founding member of The Big Carrot, I had seen it grow from a 2,000-square-foot store run co-operatively by five unemployed people in 1983 to a 8,000-square-foot supermarket with a staff of 65 eight years later. Anything seemed possible during those days and I was ready for a new challenge. The Big Carrot customers are generally middle and upper income people interested in organic food and I was curious to see how my food and customer experience would relate to this new venture.

The business started with a travelling food truck, loaded with fresh fruits and vegetables, which pulled into 20 neighbourhoods once a week on a regular schedule. Field to Table evolved into a nonprofit produce distributor selling to school food programs, pre-order groups and community markets.

Our latest and most successful venture is called The Good Food Box. With this program, we encourage people to get together and each buy a $15 share at the beginning of the month. Our job is to put together a box of the best-quality in-season fruits and vegetables and get the best value for our customers. In the third week of the month, when people are often out of food and money, we deliver a 30-to 50-pound box of produce. About 25 volunteers spend a wonderful day packing the boxes. Our only criterion is that the communities themselves must organize a group of at least 10 households, collect the money, arrange the delivery spot and receive the boxes on delivery day. The beauty of this system is that since everything is ordered ahead and pre-paid, there is no waste, unlike the standard food system, where waste is rampant.

Working with Field to Table has meant learning, adjusting and re-evaluating for me. Many ideas I had about people and food have been challenged. I discovered that for many low-income people, food is not the second priority after rent, as I expected. Paying the electricity bill is more important than buying food and when emergencies occur, the grocery budget is often the only place to cut. My own diet and shopping patterns have changed. I am much more aware of eating local in-season food and getting value for my food dollar by eating at home and preparing food from scratch. Food has always been a source of joy and a daily cause for celebration for me. But in my job now, I see that women often find food a source of anxiety and stress.

The most exciting part of my job has been meeting so many people, living in very different circumstances from my own. While I often see people coping with seemingly insurmountable problems, there is energy and vitality and hope in the more than 50 communities we serve. I share friendships across cultural, language and class barriers that I don't often cross in my own neighbourhood and there seems to be acceptance and a place for everyone.

A TRIP TO THE FOOD TERMINAL

Last year my job was to go to the Ontario Food Terminal three mornings a week to purchase wholesale cases of fruit and vegetables for customers of Field to Table.

I never sleep well the night before my buying day at the Terminal. The market starts preparing for buyers at 3 a.m. I toss and turn for a few more hours before setting out with the tools of my trade: cheques, cash, invoices, a calculator, a working ballpoint pen and yesterday's prices memorized. If I forget any one of these things, my morning will be ruined.

Produce from all over the world comes into the terminal and goes out to cities and small towns all over Ontario. The low-rise concrete block buildings form a horseshoe shape in a huge paved parking lot that's several city blocks square. Powerful individual distributors (called houses) occupy the storefronts and on the floor are skids of produce, with one case of each fruit or vegetable open for display. Transport trailers from all over North America unload at the back door and customers and small orders go in and out the front.

Each house specializes in some aspect of the produce business. Morris Brown built his reputation on tomatoes, and now his son runs the business. Meloripe specializes in tropical fruits, and some mornings the sweet smell of mangoes perfumes the air. Here you can buy hairy taro potatoes, Scotch bonnet peppers (the hottest peppers in the world), plantains and giant yellow yams packed in sawdust from Jamaica. King and Raphael attracts restaurant buyers with their exotic greens and tiny perfect vegetables. You get to know that only two places sell fresh basil, that mushrooms are at the back of Ontario Produce and that hydroponic lettuce is available only on Friday, so you need to reserve it.

Outside in the open, no matter what the weather, individual farmers and packing houses claim their strip of pavement to sell local produce. Here there's a perpetual traffic jam of trucks, with the intensity of the chaos depending on the day of the week.

I love buying locally grown food with its distinct seasonal flow: flowers at Christmas and Easter, bedding plants in spring, spotlessly clean hand-tied bunches of green onions and local bok choy, asparagus in May, corn and broccoli mid-summer, tiny delicate apricots in August and in September, pears. As well, there are greenhouse tomatoes and cucumbers from Leamington in every month except December and January. About the only local produce available year-round are apples, carrots and potatoes.

There is always too much or too little. Unlike manufactured products where inventories are just-in-time, nature resists control.

The buyers, who are mostly owners of independent grocery stores or small chains, arrive on schedule in costume. The important men who negotiate, but never load, favour trench coats and suits while the rest of us go for warm grubby clothes. Theoretically, no money changes hands before 6:30. After that, prices go up and down hourly. Drought in California, hurricanes in Florida, early frost, transportation strikes, guerrilla activities in South America, the mood of the salesperson, the time of year and the customer's smile all affect the price. Deals are made for one case or for a transport truckload, loads are assembled and shipped out.

I try to get there at 6:30 on the first bus of the day. I often find myself with the few other women walking from the bus stop in the dark and cold through the chainlink gate with its sign saying "Public not allowed." There's a shared feeling of circumstance that I have with these strangers, like the knowledge when you're up nursing your baby in the middle of the night that other women are up as well.

The terminal itself is a very male place. Young men race their pump trucks, vying to be first up and down the ramps, delivering cases and boxes to the waiting trucks. The air is blue with the F-word and posters of nude women in offices catch my attention in the middle of conversations.

True, in the restaurant there are the three waitresses who serve everything from scrambled eggs to beef stroganoff at 6:30. There's the line of dignified elderly ladies standing on the wet floor, who pack spinach with their rubber-gloved hands while the machine clicks, weighs and closes the bags we buy so thoughtlessly. Then there are the women who never make mistakes, extending invoices and adding bills in their tiny cage-like offices. I've seen only four saleswomen in all the houses and the occasional woman outside in the farmers market. As for female buyers, we're a rarity. I always smile when I see the one woman owner race recklessly by on her forklift, cigarette dangling from her mouth.

Gradually you find the salesman who will give you that 50 cents off a case, the owners who will warn you away from poor-quality peppers and the farmers who have perfect, unwaxed apples that no one else wants because they are tiny, but which our school cooks love for the midmorning snack programs.

Every morning, if I finish before our truck arrives to load, I start figuring out the prices and preparing the invoices. Of course, I always see a better price or the perfect case of broccoli, but it's too late. In the restaurant, which reminds me of those men-only Italian cafés, I never feel entirely comfortable, but now fully awake, I claim the third seat from the end at the counter for my morning coffee.

M.L.M.

GARDEN FARE

CUSTOMERS OF FIELD TO TABLE like iceberg lettuce. I buy it reluctantly every week, wishing I could get them to try romaine, buttercrunch, chicory, green leaf, red oakleaf, mâche, watercress, radicchio, Belgian endive, escarole, curly endive, dandelion or arugula. These lettuces can be mixed and matched for colour and flavour but they are fragile and expensive.

The ideal solution is to have a few pots on the balcony or a tiny square of garden for your own daily harvest. Every Italian, Portuguese, Spanish and Chinese store in the city has packs of exotic seeds with planting instructions in at least four languages. In English they begin, "After having worked in depth the soil, sow, bearing in mind ..."

The robust leaves of romaine can hold the weight and power of a Caesar dressing. Dandelion, tomatoes and onions in a simple olive oil and vinegar dressing are a spring tonic and blood cleanser. A few red radicchio leaves in a salad add to the festive air at Christmas. Arugula and watercress lend a peppery bite. One endive can change a whole salad.

In our family we eat salad after the main course. We rarely have dessert these days, so it makes a good clean ending to the meal. We've had many memorable salads including ones made with mysterious ingredients. My husband and I once shared an unforgettable salad in a family trattoria in Verona and through mime and much laughter, the couple at the next table translated the name of the tiny greens as monk's whiskers.

In Mediterranean countries, where olive oil is revered, the olive tree is a symbol of peace, fertility and purification. History records that olive trees were cultivated as long ago as 3,000 B.C. Extra-virgin oil, made from the first pressing of olives, can be bought in Italy in bulk or in bottles at farm gates in late November. The taste and colour changes from the south to the north, but by Italian law, extra-virgin oil must contain less than 1% acid.

In our grocery and specialty stores, dozens of different olive oils are available all year long, varying in colour, aroma, flavour, method of processing and country of origin. The idea is to find one suited to your taste that's not too expensive. I use extra-virgin olive oil almost exclusively on green salads but some people prefer canola (originally called Canada oil), safflower, sunflower or corn oil.

Just pour oil over the salad, toss and then sprinkle with vinegar and toss again. It takes a little practice to get the proportions right. Three parts of oil to one of vinegar is about right. If you're uncomfortable with this casual method, see the dressing recipe on page 90 for a no-fail approach.

My favourite vinegar is made from apple cider, preferably sold in a glass bottle with the "mother," or bacterial agent, in it. I also have balsamic and red wine vinegar on hand for different tastes. Balsamic vinegar is aged in a series of wooden casks — chestnut, oak, then mulberry — to give it that exquisite flavour.

The tremendous care involved in creating balsamic vinegar is only one example of the pride and craft involved in food production in Europe. Other examples are tomatoes sold on-the-vine that are on the market for only two weeks each year and local foods such as unpasteurized cheeses that are available only in particular regions and aren't exported.

On the other hand, in Canada, where we grow superior apples, flavourful lean beef and world-renowned durum wheat, the emphasis is on uniformity, efficiency and shipping commodities to the mass market.

There are very few Canadian foods that give character to a place and involve a community, with the obvious exceptions of maple syrup and the regional wineries, which are building international reputations for themselves. However, a Canadian grass-roots movement initiated by young chefs, such as Michael Stadtländer, is focusing on preparing locally grown, fresh food served in season. At Michael and Nobuyo Stadtländer's farmhouse near Collingwood, Ontario, guests can feast on such dishes as a warm salad of rosy-red grilled duck, beets, Boston red lettuce, threads of apple-cider-candied red cabbage and toasted walnuts. Chefs such as Stadtländer are part of a lively national culinary network that is being formed to celebrate and promote regional cuisine.

The recipes that follow can form a light meal when served with bread and wine or they can be simply one of several dishes in a meal. Of course, they should complement the colours and flavours of other dishes they're served with. Your own traditions will determine when you serve the salad.

M.L.M.

Asparagus & Egg Salad

This is the first spring vegetable available in our area in early May. It needs warm days to heat up the soil and magically grows inches overnight. The season is a short one, so at least twice a week we have a meal of this asparagus salad, with crusty rolls and glasses of white wine. I confess that two of us share three pounds of asparagus at a sitting. Although asparagus is now available most of the year from as far away as Peru and Chile, there is something special about waiting for the first local taste of spring.

1 lb asparagus *500 g*
3 Tbsp olive oil *45 mL*
4 tsp lemon juice or cider vinegar *20 mL*
1 hard-boiled egg, cut in eighths
salt and pepper

Wash asparagus by soaking in cold water for a few minutes. Take stalk near the end with both hands and snap. It will break so that the remaining portion of the stalk is the tender part. Boil or steam until just tender, about 5 minutes.

While asparagus is hot drizzle with olive oil. Turn gently. Drizzle with lemon juice. Salt and pepper to taste. Cut the egg into the salad. Turn gently so that egg becomes coated with oil. Serve warm or cold.

Makes 2 to 3 servings.

DANDELION SALAD

If you want to pick your own dandelions for salad, find a field that has not been sprayed and pick before the blossoms come out. After that, the leaves turn bitter. Cut the whole plant out of the ground and wash and sort through at home. Huge stalks of commercially grown dandelions are generally available year-round in supermarkets.

4 cups dandelion leaves *1 L*
½ small red or white onion, cut in crescents
1 tomato, cut in eighths (optional)
Oil and Vinegar Dressing (see page 90)

Wash dandelion greens and rip by hand into bite-sized pieces. Toss with onion and tomato (if using).

Drizzle with *Oil and Vinegar Dressing* and serve immediately.

Makes 4 to 6 servings.

MARINATED FIDDLEHEADS

Fiddleheads are the unfurled shoots of the fern plant.
This wild plant is sometimes available imported from the
Atlantic provinces. Fiddleheads are extremely fragile and
should only be bought if they are bright green. They need
to be thoroughly soaked, agitating the water with your
hands to force any brown casings off, and the ends must be
trimmed with a knife. If you pick your own in the wild,
be sure to harvest only a few from each clump to ensure
their survival. A once-a-year treat, this dish
keeps well overnight.

1 lb fiddleheads *500 g*
6 green onions
6 Tbsp lemon juice *90 mL*
2 Tbsp safflower or a mild vegetable oil *25 mL*
salt

Boil fiddleheads in water to cover for 8 minutes and drain
thoroughly.

Cut green onions into ½ inch (1 cm) pieces.

Mix lemon juice and oil and pour over vegetables. Serve
cold.

Makes 4 to 6 servings.

PICKLED WHITE RADISH

Huge long white radishes, or Japanese daikon, are now grown locally in Ontario and available in specialty grocery stores. The crisp clean flavour is a good balance with meat dishes.

½ giant white radish
1 carrot
1 tsp salt *5 mL*
½ cup cold water *125 mL*
1 tsp sugar *5 mL*
1 Tbsp white vinegar *15 mL*

Grate radish coarsely. Cut carrot into thin strips about 3 inches (8 cm) long.

Combine vegetables in a bowl and rub salt into radish and carrot. Add water and let stand 30 minutes.

Rinse vegetables well and drain. Sprinkle with sugar. Stir in vinegar.

Makes 6 to 8 servings as a side salad.

CUCUMBER SALAD

This salad requires virtually no time to put together.
For a meal in a hurry, put burgers on the barbeque and
serve Cucumber Salad *on the side. It's a refreshingly*
cool summer salad, and a wonderful addition
to a picnic menu.

2 cucumbers
¼ red onion
½ cup yogurt or sour cream *125 mL*
1 Tbsp lemon juice *15 mL*
1½ tsp chopped fresh dill *7 mL*
salt and white pepper

Peel, seed and thinly slice cucumbers.
Cut onion into thin strips.
Whisk together yogurt and lemon juice in bowl. Stir in
vegetables and dill. Sprinkle with salt and pepper.

Makes 4 servings.

▼ ▼ ▼ ▼ ▼ ▼ ▼ ▼ ▼ ▼ ▼ ▼ ▼ ▼ ▼

CUCUMBERS

Cucumbers have an ancient history in Asia
and Africa — going back about 3,000 years.
Now many different varieties are grown
around the world. European and English
cucumbers are smooth skinned, while
Japanese and Chinese cucumbers are ridged
and rough. Most are mild flavoured. Small,
immature cucumbers can be harvested for
pickling, although special varieties can also be
grown for that purpose.

The skin of the cucumber you choose should
be green and the flesh firm whether you're
making pickles or salads. Cucumbers can contain a lot of moisture, and if the season has
been particularly wet, you may want to
remove some moisture before making your
salad. Slice the cucumber thinly and squeeze
between clean tea towels; this will allow the
cucumber to absorb dressing, instead of dilut-
ing it. A dry growing season, on the other
hand, may produce rather bitter cucumbers.
Taste them before adding to your salad. Some
people like mature (yellowing) cucumbers
cooked, much like summer squash, but they
should be peeled and seeded first.

▲ ▲ ▲ ▲ ▲ ▲ ▲ ▲ ▲ ▲ ▲ ▲ ▲ ▲ ▲

Garden Salad with Basil Vinaigrette

You can make your own basil vinegar following the instructions for making vinegar on page 106.

¼ *cup* basil vinegar *50 mL*
¼ *cup* olive oil *50 mL*
2 *to 3* tomatoes, cut in wedges
1 cucumber, seeded and sliced
½ red onion, cut into rings
⅓ *cup* chopped fresh parsley *75 mL*

Whisk vinegar and oil in salad bowl.
Add tomatoes, cucumber, red onion and parsley, tossing to coat.

Makes 4 servings

CUCUMBER & TOMATO SALAD

English cucumbers have very small seeds and a mild flavour. They are grown under glass with few sprays and harvested and shrink-wrapped in plastic. This keeps the cucumbers in excellent form and avoids the wax that now coats all field cucumbers, peppers, eggplants and most apples to extend their storage life.

½ English cucumber, sliced
3 tomatoes, cored and cut into eighths
1 small onion, diced (optional)
½ *cup* chick peas (optional) *125 mL*
¼ *cup* olives (optional) *50 mL*
3 *Tbsp* olive oil *45 mL*
4 *tsp* balsamic or wine vinegar *20 mL*

Combine vegetables. Pour olive oil and vinegar over vegetables and toss.

Makes 4 servings.

MARINATED TOMATOES

Basil leaves, plucked fresh from the herb garden, rinsed gently to avoid bruising and patted dry, add a delicate flavour and marvellous fragrance to this dish.

4 large tomatoes, sliced
basil leaves
2 *Tbsp* icing sugar *25 mL*
1 *tsp* salt *5 ml*
¼ *tsp* pepper *1 mL*
¼ *cup* vinegar *50 mL*

Slice tomatoes into shallow dish or picnic container, tucking basil between slices.

Sprinkle with sugar, salt and pepper. Drizzle with vinegar.

Keep at room temperature until serving time.

Makes 4 to 6 servings.

▼ ▼ ▼ ▼ ▼ ▼ ▼ ▼ ▼ ▼ ▼ ▼ ▼ ▼ ▼

BASIL

In Italy and India, basil is a perennial, but it's
tender and cannot survive even a hint of frost.
In Canada, growing basil in pots allows it to
be moved indoors onto windowsills when
evenings turn cool. Grown among the tomatoes, its fragrance is said to offend tomato
pests, thereby protecting its companion.

▲ ▲ ▲ ▲ ▲ ▲ ▲ ▲ ▲ ▲ ▲ ▲ ▲ ▲ ▲

▼ ▼ ▼ ▼ ▼ ▼ ▼ ▼ ▼ ▼ ▼ ▼ ▼ ▼ ▼

TOMATOES

Like basil, tomatoes are thought to have
aphrodisiac powers. But during the 16th century, Europeans thought the Aztecs' xtomatle
was poisonous, because it's a relative of the
deadly nightshade. Over time, however,
tomatoes became increasingly popular, eventually making their way back to the Americas.
Tomatoes are high in nutrients — particularly
vitamins A and C, phosphorus and potassium
— and low in calories. When they're ripe,
tomatoes can simply be sliced and served as a
side dish or in a sandwich; green, they make
delicious pickles, relishes and chutney.

▲ ▲ ▲ ▲ ▲ ▲ ▲ ▲ ▲ ▲ ▲ ▲ ▲ ▲ ▲

Spinach & Sprout Salad with Honey Dressing

If you carry your salad bowl to the garden when clipping salad greens, you'll always have the perfect amount of greens. Honey Dressing *is also excellent on fruit salads.*

spinach
1 cup alfalfa sprouts *250 mL*
1 cup sliced mushrooms *250 mL*
1/2 cup feta cheese chunks *125 mL*
2 Tbsp poppy seeds *25 mL*

Honey Dressing
½ cup liquid honey *125 mL*
¼ cup hot water *50 mL*
¼ cup lemon juice *50 mL*
¼ cup oil *50 mL*
¼ tsp salt *1 mL*
¼ tsp ground ginger *1 mL*
dash ground cloves

For Honey Dressing, blend ingredients well in a shaker or hand mixer.

Wash and spin spinach leaves and tear into large bowl.

Add alfalfa sprouts, sliced mushrooms and chunks of feta cheese to taste.

Toss with ½ cup (125 mL) HONEY DRESSING and sprinkle with poppy seeds just before serving.

Makes 4 to 6 servings

▼ ▼ ▼ ▼ ▼ ▼ ▼ ▼ ▼ ▼ ▼ ▼ ▼ ▼ ▼

HONEY

Honey is one of the sweetest of sweeteners. Unlike ordinary sugar, honey brings the flavour and aroma of a summer meadow to the table. Clover honey, a mild variety generally favoured by most people, is recommended for this recipe. Occasionally, you may find wildflower or orchard blossom honey, which is also mild. Buckwheat honey, on the other hand, is darker in colour and heavier in flavour. A good substitute for molasses, it's best in heavy cakes and dense dessert breads. If you're substituting a cup of honey for a cup of sugar, reduce the liquid in a recipe by about one-quarter cup. When substituting honey for sugar in recipes, remember that it burns more easily during baking and requires a moderate (325° to 350°F/160° to 180°C) oven.

▲ ▲ ▲ ▲ ▲ ▲ ▲ ▲ ▲ ▲ ▲ ▲ ▲ ▲ ▲ ▲

LEMON DRESSING

Tangy and easy, serve it on a simple leafy green salad.

⅓ cup lemon juice *75 mL*
2 tsp lemon pepper *10 mL*
2 sliced green onions or shallots
½ tsp salt *2 mL*
1 cup olive oil *250 mL*

In food processor, pour lemon juice, lemon pepper, shallots and salt. With motor running, slowly add olive oil. Dress a mixed leafy green salad before serving.

Makes 1⅓ cups.

▼ ▼ ▼ ▼ ▼ ▼ ▼ ▼ ▼ ▼ ▼ ▼ ▼ ▼ ▼ ▼

OILS

Canola is the lowest in saturated fat and one of the mildest tasting of all the oils. Olive oil is popular for sautéing and for salads. Flavours vary considerably — from fruity-flavoured extra-virgin (a good salad choice) to darker more robust flavours.

▲ ▲ ▲ ▲ ▲ ▲ ▲ ▲ ▲ ▲ ▲ ▲ ▲ ▲ ▲

GREEN BEANS VINAIGRETTE

This vinaigrette is delicious with potatoes but best with beans. For colour, add sliced mushrooms, slivers of red pepper or red onions or tiny pieces of lemon.

1 lb green beans *500 g*
3 Tbsp olive oil *45 mL*
1 Tbsp Dijon mustard *15 mL*
4 tsp lemon juice or cider vinegar *20 mL*
salt and pepper

Tail and cut ends off beans. Steam until just tender, about 5 minutes. Drain thoroughly and put into bowl.

While beans are hot, stir in olive oil and mustard. Toss gently. Drizzle with lemon juice. Salt and pepper to taste.

Serve warm or cold.

Makes 3 to 4 servings.

OIL & VINEGAR DRESSING

*Experiment with different oils and vinegars until you
find a combination that suits your taste. This dressing can
be stored for up to 2 weeks in the refrigerator.*

½ cup oil *125 mL*
3 Tbsp wine vinegar or lemon juice *45 mL*
1 Tbsp Dijon mustard *15 mL*
3 cloves garlic, minced
salt and pepper

Shake ingredients together in small jar.

Makes ¾ cup (175 mL). Can be easily doubled.

MARINATED SUMMER SALAD

This salad stores well for up to a week, allowing flavours
a chance to ripen. Store covered in the fridge, stirring
occasionally to keep the vegetables coated with
the marinade.

1 head cauliflower, cut into florets
4 carrots, sliced into matchsticks
2 green peppers, sliced
4 celery stalks, sliced
½ cup pimiento-stuffed olives *125 mL*
1½ cups vinegar *375 mL*
1 cup olive oil *250 mL*
½ cup sugar *125 mL*
¾ tsp oregano leaves *4 mL*
1 tsp salt *5 mL*
½ tsp pepper *2 mL*

Combine all ingredients in saucepan, cover and bring to
boil. Simmer 5 minutes.

Refrigerate overnight. Drain before serving.

Makes 6 to 8 servings.

▼ ▼ ▼ ▼ ▼ ▼ ▼ ▼ ▼ ▼ ▼ ▼ ▼ ▼ ▼ ▼

CAULIFLOWER

Raw, the florets make a delicious addition to a vegetable platter. To serve as a side dish, boil florets gently until just fork-tender, about 10 minutes. In order to retain the crisp white colour of the florets during cooking, add a teaspoon of vinegar to every two cups of water. To serve, drain, then dust with freshly grated pepper. Although cheese sauce is a tasty traditional topping for cauliflower, it adds calories. Without any sauce, cauliflower contains only 25 to 30 calories per cup.

▲ ▲ ▲ ▲ ▲ ▲ ▲ ▲ ▲ ▲ ▲ ▲ ▲ ▲ ▲ ▲

RAW BEET &
CARROT SALAD

This salad also tastes great the next day. Beets contain vitamins A and C. We normally think of imported citrus fruits and juices as our best source of vitamin C, but it's possible to get all we need from locally grown food.

2 beets, peeled
2 carrots, peeled
2 Tbsp olive oil *25 mL*
4 tsp balsamic vinegar *20 mL*
salt and pepper

Grate carrots and beets on fine side of grater or use a food processor.

Add oil and vinegar and toss gently. Add salt and pepper to taste.

Makes 4 servings.

BEET TOPS VINAIGRETTE

*Beets in bunches at the supermarket produce counter are
another sign of spring. The tops, which contain vitamins
A and C and calcium, are a special treat and
shouldn't be discarded.*

1 bunch beet tops
1 Tbsp butter *15 mL*
2 Tbsp apple cider vinegar *25 mL*
salt and pepper

Boil beet tops for 10 minutes. Drain; stir in butter.
Drizzle with apple cider vinegar. Salt and pepper to taste.
Serve warm.

Makes 2 servings.

BERNIE'S COLESLAW

This recipe is a particular favourite because it recalls family gatherings — and because it keeps up to 3 weeks in the fridge. In fact, it improves as time goes by.

1 large cabbage, shredded
1 green pepper, chopped
1 sweet onion, diced
⅔ cup vegetable oil *150 mL*
1 cup sugar *250 mL*
1 tsp dry mustard *5 mL*
1 tsp celery seed *5 mL*
1 tsp salt *5 mL*
1 cup cider vinegar *250 mL*

Mix vegetables in large bowl.

In saucepan, bring remaining ingredients to boil. Remove from heat, and pour over cabbage mixture.

Allow coleslaw to come to room temperature before covering and refrigerating.

Makes 8 to 10 servings.

▼ ▼ ▼ ▼ ▼ ▼ ▼ ▼ ▼ ▼ ▼ ▼ ▼ ▼ ▼ ▼

CABBAGE

Most cabbages are light green in colour, but
the Savoy is dark green and crinkly. Although
raw cabbage is generally eaten in salads, it can
be cooked by steaming, sautéing or stir-
frying. It can also be braised in the oven, or
added to soups shortly before serving. But it
shouldn't be boiled rapidly in lots of water;
this causes its sulphur compounds to break
down, creating a nasty odour. Like its relatives, broccoli and Brussels sprouts, cabbage
is a full-flavoured vegetable and is best
when freshly harvested.

▲ ▲ ▲ ▲ ▲ ▲ ▲ ▲ ▲ ▲ ▲ ▲ ▲ ▲ ▲ ▲

BRAISED CABBAGE & APPLE

*Cabbages and apples, both plentiful in the autumn,
combine to make a fine braised dish.*

1 tsp vegetable oil *5 mL*
½ Tbsp honey *7 mL*
½ onion, finely chopped
2 cups sliced cored peeled apples *500 mL*
2 cups shredded cabbage *500 mL*
1 Tbsp vinegar *15 mL*
2 tsp caraway seeds *10 mL*

Heat oil in skillet over medium heat; stir in honey.
Sauté onion until softened.

Stir in apples, cabbage, vinegar and caraway seeds; cook
until tender, about 30 minutes.

Makes 4 servings

▼

BRUSCHETTA

The proper bread is important for this great company appetizer. In a pinch, a French stick will do, but flat oval-shaped Toscana bread is ideal. In Tuscany, little boys eat their crusts and avoid the middle of the bread.

1   Toscana bread or French stick
4   tomatoes, chopped
3 Tbsp olive oil *45 mL*
3   cloves garlic, minced
1 Tbsp chopped fresh parsley or basil *15 mL*
salt and pepper
Parmesan cheese (optional)

Cut bread in thin slices and toast lightly under broiler.
Mix tomatoes, oil, garlic, parsley and salt and pepper.
Spread toast with tomato mixture so that all edges are covered, and sprinkle with grated Parmesan cheese (if using).
Broil again until tomatoes begin to sweat, about 3 minutes. Serve hot.

Makes 4 appetizers or 2 lunch servings.

OVEN-BAKED
EGGPLANT SLICES

In combination with Marinated Red Peppers, *this makes an unbeatable sandwich. Eggplant soaks up oil if it is fried, broiling or baking is a healthier and easier cooking method. There are many varieties of eggplant — the egg-shaped, violet Sicilian eggplant, the small white Chinese eggplant and the familiar glossy black globes. The seeds can give a bitter taste so many recipes suggest salting the slices and letting them sit in a colander for half an hour before washing and proceeding. Buy firm, shiny fresh eggplant to avoid this problem.*

3 large black eggplants
olive oil
thyme, pepper and oregano (optional)

Slice eggplant lengthwise into pieces 1 inch (2.5 cm) thick. Brush 2 baking sheets lightly with olive oil. Place eggplant slices on sheets. Brush tops lightly with oil. Sprinkle with thyme, pepper and oregano if you wish. Bake 20 minutes at 350°F (180°C). Turn once and cook another 20 minutes until brown and soft. Cool. Can be stored, covered, in refrigerator for several days.

Makes 6 to 8 servings.

MARINATED RED PEPPERS

There are only a few weeks of the year in late August and September when red peppers are affordable for this extravagant dish. Watch for markdowns on the produce shelf the rest of the time. This dish can be served as a splash of colour on the plate (a forkful is enough) or as a sandwich filling on a crusty roll.

8 sweet red peppers
6 cloves garlic, minced
½ cup olive oil *125 mL*
4 Tbsp vinegar or lemon juice *60 mL*
salt and pepper

Seed and halve red peppers. Place peppers skin side down on hot barbeque. Close lid and cook until the skin is charred black. Or place peppers skin side up on baking sheets and broil close to the heating element until skin bubbles and chars.

Put hot peppers into sturdy paper bag. (The steam created forces skin to separate from pepper.)

When cool, skin each pepper. Cut peppers into strips and place in bowl. Stir in remaining ingredients and let marinate.

This keeps well, covered, in the refrigerator for at least 1 week. Any leftover marinade adds excellent flavour to other salads.

Makes 2 cups (500 mL).

▼

PESTO

This fresh basil sauce is delicious served over pasta or cooked potatoes or spread on a pizza instead of cheese and tomatoes. Pesto can be refrigerated for weeks if the surface is covered with olive oil. It can also be frozen in small containers or ice-cube trays and these tiny cubes can be added to soups for extra flavour. If the pesto is to be frozen for later use, leave out the Parmesan and add it just before serving. The story of pesto's creation is that a sailor cook used the wild basil that flourished in the shipyards of Genoa to make pesto for returning sailors who were yearning for fresh greens after months of a shipboard diet.

2 *cups* packed fresh basil leaves *500 mL*
4 *Tbsp* pine nuts or blanched almonds *60 mL*
3 cloves garlic
salt
¾ *cup* olive oil *175 mL*
½ *cup* grated Parmesan cheese (optional) *125 mL*

Blend basil, pine nuts, garlic and salt in blender or food processor.

Slowly drizzle in olive oil while machine is running. Blend in parmesan cheese until smooth.

Makes enough for 1 lh (500 g) pasta.

GEORGIA'S GREEK SALAD

The ingredients in this salad can vary, depending on what's in season, but the essential items are tasty tomatoes, black olives, onions, feta cheese, olive oil, oregano and lemon juice or vinegar. Georgia Nayyar teaches nutrition and cooking skills to a group of women who cook together in an inner-city community kitchen.

1 head lettuce (optional)
½ cucumber, thinly sliced
4 tomatoes, sliced
1 sweet onion, sliced
12 sprigs fresh mint
4 Tbsp olive oil *60 mL*
3 Tbsp lemon juice or vinegar *45 mL*
1 Tbsp oregano *15 mL*
½ cup crumbled feta cheese *125 mL*
20 black Kalamata olives

Roll the lettuce leaves and slice thinly with a stainless steel knife. Scatter over large serving platter.

Arrange cucumber, tomatoes, onion rings and mint on top.

Mix oil, lemon juice and oregano. Pour over salad. Sprinkle with feta cheese and olives.

Makes 4 to 6 servings.

▼ ▼ ▼ ▼ ▼ ▼ ▼ ▼ ▼ ▼ ▼ ▼ ▼ ▼ ▼ ▼

FETA CHEESE

Feta cheese was originally made with sheep or
goat's milk and cured in a salt brine. Today,
it's often made with a mixture of milks,
including cow's milk. We can buy feta
imported in huge tins from Greece and
Denmark and also purchase locally made
cheese, whose creamy flavour surpasses all. Its
sharp, salty flavour goes perfectly with black
Kalamata olives.

▲ ▲ ▲ ▲ ▲ ▲ ▲ ▲ ▲ ▲ ▲ ▲ ▲ ▲ ▲ ▲ ▲

SALAD NIÇOISE

*We always get a craving for this complete meal salad in
the summer. This recipe started out as Julia Child's but
has been simplified and modified. New potatoes need a
longer cooking time than older potatoes.*

4 new potatoes
1 lb green beans, trimmed *500 g*
¾ cup Oil and Vinegar Dressing (see page 90) *175 mL*
1 Tbsp Dijon mustard *15 mL*
3 tomatoes, quartered
½ cup Kalamata olives *125 mL*
1 hard-boiled egg (optional)
1 can (7.5 oz /213 g) chunk white tuna, drained
1 Tbsp capers *15 mL*
½ head romaine lettuce

Cut potatoes into chunks. Cook in boiling water until
tender, about 15 minutes. Steam beans until tender, about 5
minutes. Put warm cooked potatoes and beans in bowl. Toss
with ½ cup (125 mL) *Oil and Vinegar Dressing* and Dijon
mustard. Let sit for 10 minutes.

Add tomatoes, olives, egg, tuna and capers. Toss gently.

Line large salad bowl with torn romaine lettuce. Add
other vegetables. Sprinkle with remaining dressing.

Makes 4 servings.

FOUR-BEAN SALAD

This salad is even better the next day and travels well to work or school. Colours are important. Cut the green and yellow beans into equal lengths and cut the red pepper into triangular shapes for contrast.

1 *lb* fresh green beans *500 g*
1 *lb* fresh yellow beans *500 g*
1 can (19 oz/540 mL) chick peas, drained and rinsed
1 can (19 oz/540 mL) kidney beans, drained and rinsed
1 onion, minced
½ sweet red pepper, seeded and cut
⅓ *cup* olive oil *75 mL*
⅓ *cup* wine vinegar *75 mL*
salt and pepper
3 *Tbsp* chopped parsley *45 mL*

Trim green and yellow beans and cut into 2 inch (5 cm) lengths.

Steam beans until barely tender, about 4 minutes. Immerse in cold water to stop cooking. Drain.

Put in bowl with chick peas, kidney beans, onion and red pepper and stir in oil and vinegar.

Salt and pepper to taste. Toss gently and sprinkle with parsley.

Makes 4 main course or 8 side-dish servings.

▼

▼ ▼ ▼ ▼ ▼ ▼ ▼ ▼ ▼ ▼ ▼ ▼ ▼ ▼ ▼ ▼

RED RADISHES

Bunch red radishes with their prickly tops are
tempting to buy, but almost need to be tasted
before purchasing to make sure they are not
bitter. Wash them, cut off the root and leave
about an inch of the green stalk. Store in a
dish of water in the refrigerator. Serve simply,
drained but chilled in a white bowl with dark
bread, butter and salt. They make great
snacks for adults.

▲ ▲ ▲ ▲ ▲ ▲ ▲ ▲ ▲ ▲ ▲ ▲ ▲ ▲ ▲ ▲ ▲

▼ ▼ ▼ ▼ ▼ ▼ ▼ ▼ ▼ ▼ ▼ ▼ ▼ ▼ ▼ ▼

MAKING VINEGARS

Select unblemished, fresh herbs — they're
best picked early in the day when the dew is
still on them. Wash gently and pat dry. Slip 2
or 3 stalks into a glass bottle with a stopper
or cork — basil in one bottle, tarragon in
another, for example. Pour good-quality
white wine vinegar over the herbs. Cork
and put in a sunny window for a couple of
weeks to mature, tasting periodically until
you like the flavour. Strain and rebottle.
Either put a small sprig of herb into the
bottle or label it to identify.

▲ ▲ ▲ ▲ ▲ ▲ ▲ ▲ ▲ ▲ ▲ ▲ ▲ ▲ ▲ ▲ ▲

HEARTY MEALS

FARMING AND FOOD: SEEKING THE FUTURE

LIKE MOST FARM FAMILIES, mine had nurtured a huge garden. From early spring through late fall, the garden supplied most of our table needs, while the cash crop farming my father did provided necessary dollars to keep farm and family intact.

Rhubarb sprouted in the spring, leading to pies and rhubarb-and-strawberry jam. Lettuces, green onions, radishes — a full array of salad fixings — grew in the garden. We weeded beans, corn, peas and squash. We grew potatoes, carrots, turnips, parsnips and other root vegetables. We harvested raspberries, and red and black currants from the bushes in my Aunt Julia's side yard. My mother planted zinnia seeds saved from the previous year's flowers, and their colourful heads bobbed along the garden path between our houses. The women canned, dried and tucked foods into root cellars. They augmented their garden harvests with fruits grown in nearby orchards. And after my own children were born, Aunt Julia came with us to pick windfalls from beneath the apple trees and sat at my kitchen table preparing them for applesauce.

My children are grown. Life seems to have accelerated to an incredible pace — one that makes my childhood seem idyllic. But it would be inaccurate to leave the impression that my parents' or my grandparents' lives were slow and easy. They worked incredibly hard over long hours.

Once, the farm family supplied most of the labour required to prepare the soil, sow, tend and harvest crops. Until recently, haying season meant that throughout June and early July wagon load after wagon load of baled hay was hauled from fields, transferred into lofts above stables and barn floors where it was stored for livestock feed during the winter. But machines have largely replaced the labour of women, men and children. Now, balers wrap and tie hay into 700-pound round bales instead of the 70-pound bales that required so much labour. With the new technology, one operator can do the work that used to require a crew of six or more.

Farmers are driven to compete and in our attempts to establish productive and efficient modern farms, we've exchanged one yoke for another. The toll taken by physical exertion has been replaced by the stress resulting from the higher capital costs required to pay for sophisticated and expensive equipment — a necessity on today's farms.

Agriculture has become capital-intensive big business. The pressure to be efficient has driven farmers to become larger and more specialized or to leave farming. In this way, farmers step onto the technology treadmill, extending themselves financially — in the name of efficiency, productivity and competitiveness.

Those who stepped off the treadmill created an exodus from rural Canada. Following the Second World War, about 18 percent of the Canadian population lived on farms. By 1961, the farm population had dropped to just over 12 percent. By 1981, approximately 4 percent lived on farms, and by 1991, only 2 percent of Canadians did. But despite the dramatic decline in the number of farm families, productivity has actually increased.

During this period, costs for machinery, fuel, hybrid seeds and so on have skyrocketed, while most commodity prices at the farm gate are comparable to those of the Great

Depression. This has forced many growers to seek off-farm employment. The impact of technology also appears to be driving policy, which in turn, is leading us toward a new vision of agriculture.

Two models dominate our vision of farming in the future: one European and the other American. In Europe, where governments tend to provide more socialist supports, there's an emphasis on keeping rural communities, sustaining family farms and marketing unique regional produce. European agricultural policy isn't problem free, but it values a vital living countryside. The Americans, on the other hand, prize efficiency and bigness. The complex system they've developed favours corporate ownerships and partnerships, which are often vertically integrated. This means that one company might own or control research laboratories, grain elevators, feed lots, abattoirs and processing plants, effectively dominating that industry. Frequently, the farmer becomes just a link in the chain, losing independent decision-making power. A David-and-Goliath struggle is going on in the United States now between small family farms and huge agricultural conglomerates. Only, unlike the original battle, it looks as if the giant is winning.

In Canada, we seem to be leaning toward the American model. Large American conglomerates are making significant inroads into segments of the Canadian farming industry. Will we encourage locally grown food and niche marketing, as the Europeans do, or will we allow huge conglomerates to take over our farming, which could create more reliance on imported foods? Or will we achieve a uniquely Canadian solution?

The answers to these questions are critical, especially for farmers, because our livelihood is at stake. According to Statistics Canada, the average investment a farmer makes in land and machinery is about half a million dollars. And yet the average annual Canadian farm income, before assets are depreciated, is just $16,000. (After depreciation, the average annual Canadian farm income is $6,500.) To make ends meet, many members of rural families must work off the farm; the average annual income earned by them is just over $21,000, a significant contribution toward a minimum standard of living. Canadians could face a challenging future if current trends continue, because the health of the countryside and the quality and availability of food is at stake. The consequences will reach beyond farmers, touching each of us.

Another major change in farming has happened because of women's changing roles. Traditionally, farm women assumed responsibility for domestic labour, child care and care for the aged as well as on-farm labour — frequently in the fields in key periods such as planting and harvesting and daily in the barns with animal chores. In addition, women have more recently assumed farm-management roles. Now, women are working off the farm in greater numbers than ever before.

Here again, I'm part of a trend. Five days a week, I leave Whiteoaks Farm and drive 25 kilometres to an off-farm job. Like me, many rural women use their varied skills in off-farm employment in order to provide essential cash for the farm. And many women find themselves under-employed or travelling extraordinary distances for appropriate work, because of the scarce job opportunities in rural areas.

My mother raised her family, ran the home, worked on community organizations and provided support to the farm business. She used her creativity and skills in ways that society deemed appropriate. But she had little ambition to act in the political arena and accepted that farm organizations were the turf of men. By contrast, I'm participating politically. And I'm not alone. Statistics show that an increasing number of women are active in agricultural politics.

While some barriers to women in the political arena are falling, their participation on traditionally male-dominated marketing boards and in farm organizations is increasing very slowly indeed. Although some inroads are being made at the grassroots level, few women are found in the executive board-rooms of these groups. Farm women's activism has happened in two waves. The first occurred at the beginning of the century, culminating when women won the vote. The second began in 1975, during International Women's Year when the struggle to promote equality gained renewed energy. For farm women, a watershed occurred when they came together at the first National Farm Women's Conference held in Ottawa in 1980. By 1986 an informal network had been established. since then, members and affiliates from seven provinces including the Ontario Farm Women's Network to which I belong, have joined efforts. Together, these women's groups lobby to improve their representation on policy-setting boards and farm organizations and to improve the quality of life and the financial well-being of farm families. To influence future decisions, women's voices must be heard beyond the kitchen table. Our voices must be heard at policy-setting tables.

K.M.

HEARTY MEALS

NOT HAVING ENOUGH time to cook is the reality for most of us today. It's a challenge for those of us who want to provide our families with economical and nutritious meals. Mary Lou and I lament the lack of time we have to spend in our kitchens; instead, we find we often have time only to dream about cooking.

Salads are quick and simple to prepare. Choose a mix of red and green lettuce, curly endive or perhaps a little watercress. If salad is to be a complete meal in a hurry, add cubed pieces of feta, Cheddar or blue cheese. Or toss in bite-sized chunks of poached chicken breast, fish, cold roast beef or ham with the leafy greens.

Fresh vegetables can often be served raw with a dip, accompanied by sandwiches. Or steam vegetables for a few minutes until tender; then drizzle them with a teaspoon or two of white or herb vinegar, and serve with a dollop of butter and a sprinkle of freshly grated pepper to accompany broiled fish fillets.

With a little attention, vegetables can become the focal point of the meal. During harvest season when they're plentiful, they're also reasonably priced. In fact, in-season vegetables that have been grown nearby and freshly picked have the added advantage of being higher in nutrients and fuller in flavour than imported or stored produce. In May and June when asparagus is abundant, make *Springtime Cream of*

Asparagus Soup. In the summer, try *Corn & Potato Chowder* or *Gardener's Ratatouille.* In the fall, indulge yourself with *Tarragon Tomato Soup* or *Hot & Spicy Bean Soup.* One of the advantages of eating locally grown food is the variety of foods and flavours you'll enjoy over the course of a year. It does, however, require cooks to be flexible and willing to build meals around availability.

While some people choose a recipe and then purchase the ingredients to make it, others look at what they have on hand, what is growing in the garden or what is reasonably priced at the market, before reaching for a cookbook. One of our contributors, Jan Nightingale, uses this approach. "In fact, I rarely use a recipe," she says. "My favourite is what I call kitchen sink soup, using whatever is on hand."

Jan uses chicken or beef broth as a soup base, browning and simmering leftover meat to begin her soups. My mother, who was a child of the Great Depression of the 1930s, taught me to be frugal and never to throw away what might be used. Although I don't recall her making potato-peel broth, I've gone through touch-and-go economic times when I've made vegetable stock from peelings. Frugality, however, isn't the only reason for using peelings to make a soup base; most nutrients are found just below the peel, which is too often discarded. But I'd recommend using vegetables that have been grown organically, since chemical residues also tend to be greatest near the peel.

To make nutritious but frugal vegetable stock, cover scrubbed potato, carrot and other vegetable peels with water. Add stalks of cauliflower or broccoli (reserving the florets for veggie and dip platters) and the base of celery stalks, if you have them on hand. Add onion skins and seasonings to the soup pot. Simmer for an hour or so then, strain. This makes a delicious and nutritious stock for homemade soup. If you make it on a day when you are housebound, it'll be ready in the refrigerator or freezer on a day when you are too busy to cook.

Pasta, rice and lentils cook quickly and make the foundation of a good meal. Grains and lentil dishes can be dressed or marinated and served as cold salads, or combined with sauces and served hot. Potatoes are a good source of complex carbohydrates. Legumes and dried beans are a good source of protein and vitamins, and although they require long cooking times, they require little attention while they're simmering. Lentils and split peas, which are part of this food family, soften faster — taking less than an hour from start to serving.

Most of the recipes in this chapter can be made with little time spent in the kitchen, although some require simmering, which means you should be nearby. Even meals prepared with a minimum of time and fuss should provide a balance of flavours, textures and nutrients. For example, combine a crisp salad, full of vitamins, with a pita, brimming with a protein-rich filling, and you have a balanced meal.

K.M.

Springtime Cream of Asparagus Soup

Asparagus is the first vegetable of the season. Lucky are the people who know where a wild stand grows. There is a commercial asparagus farm on Wolfe Island, where Lake Ontario flows into the St. Lawrence River. A ferry ride on a sunny spring afternoon leads to a basket or two of this delectable food. On the way home, I usually eat quite a few spears, as if they were stalks of celery. Asparagus is wonderful, simply steamed. But if you want something a little more substantial, try Springtime Cream of Asparagus Soup. *In less than 30 minutes you have a wonderful meal.*

1 lb asparagus 500 g
2 cups water 500 mL
1 tsp salt 5 mL
¼ cup flour 50 mL
¼ sweet red pepper, minced (optional)
3 cups light cream 750 mL
½ cup dry white wine 125 mL
1 egg yolk (optional)
1 cup sliced mushrooms 250 mL
freshly ground pepper

Wash asparagus and snap off ends.

Cut stalks into 1 inch (2.5 cm) pieces, reserving tips.

Simmer stalks in pot of salted water until tender, 10 to 12 minutes.

Remove with slotted spoon and purée by hand or in food processor, slowly adding flour.

In asparagus cooking water, simmer tips and red pepper (if using) until tender, 3 to 5 minutes.

Whisk in purée, cream, wine and egg yolk (if using).

Cook until thickened, about 10 minutes.

Stir in mushrooms and pepper; cook for 2 minutes.

Makes 4 servings.

▼ ▼ ▼ ▼ ▼ ▼ ▼ ▼ ▼ ▼ ▼ ▼ ▼ ▼ ▼ ▼

ASPARAGUS

Asparagus is best harvested in the morning.
Select spears when the heads are tight. Cut
under the soil to protect next year's crop.
Refrigerate; asparagus wilts quickly.

▲ ▲ ▲ ▲ ▲ ▲ ▲ ▲ ▲ ▲ ▲ ▲ ▲ ▲ ▲ ▲

CUCUMBER & BUTTERMILK SOUP

It is said that the French introduced iced soups to England after the French Revolution. Iced soups must be truly chilled to bring out their subtle flavours. They combine either fruits or vegetables with stock, milk, cream, yogurt, sour cream or buttermilk. This soup requires no cooking and only minutes to prepare.

4 cups buttermilk 1 L
½ sweet green pepper, chopped
1 cucumber, sliced
salt and white pepper
4 sprigs parsley

Reserve 4 slices of cucumber and parsley for garnish.

In blender, combine 1 cup (250 mL) of the buttermilk and the remaining ingredients.

Purée at high speed until smooth. Mix well with remaining buttermilk.

Chill thoroughly.

Float cucumber slice and sprig of parsley in each serving bowl.

Makes 4 servings.

LEEK & POTATO SOUP
WITH CUCUMBERS

*Potatoes, cucumbers and leeks from the garden combine
easily and quickly in this recipe. Great served hot with
biscuits warm from the oven, this soup also makes a
superb cold lunch.*

2 Tbsp butter *25 mL*
1 large leek, chopped
4 large potatoes, peeled and cubed
3 cups water *750 mL*
1 bay leaf
2 cups light cream or milk *500 mL*
1 cup peeled, seeded and diced cucumber *250 mL*
salt and pepper
2 Tbsp chopped chives (optional) *25 mL*

Melt butter in large pot; sautée leek in butter for 5 minutes. Add potatoes, water and bay leaf; bring to a boil. Cook
until potatoes are tender, about 15 to 20 minutes. Strain the
vegetables, removing and discarding bay leaf; return broth to
pot. Purée vegetables in food processor or push through
sieve. Return to pot. Stir in cream, cucumber, salt and pepper. Sprinkle with chopped chives.

Makes 4 servings.

TARRAGON TOMATO SOUP

*This soup benefits from a late-summer garden near the
kitchen door, although all of the ingredients should be
available from your neighbourhood greengrocer if you
don't have a garden. Tarragon grows like a weed along
the wall of our woodshed, and its abundance each summer
presents quite a challenge. Rose, a neighbour who recently
moved from Germany, transplanted some of my thin-
nings into her garden, and in exchange, graciously shared
this recipe. This wonderful, chunky, full-bodied soup is
quick and easy to prepare. If you have some slightly stale
French or Italian bread, you can top the soup with homemade croutons. Pass chunks of cheese and crusty rolls
for a satisfying supper.*

2 *Tbsp* butter *25 mL*
2 *Tbsp* olive oil *25 mL*
2 onions, chopped
3 cloves garlic, diced
8 cups peeled, chopped tomatoes *2 L*
1 cup chopped fresh tarragon leaves (or other herbs, such as
marjoram, dill or parsley) *250 mL*

1 tsp honey *5 mL*
¾ tsp salt *4 mL*
¼ tsp pepper *1 mL*
3-4 Tbsp mayonnaise *45-60 mL*

In heavy skillet, heat butter and oil. Sauté onion and garlic for 5 minutes or until softened.

Stir in tomatoes, tarragon, honey, salt and pepper.

Simmer over medium heat about 15 minutes to cook the tomatoes and blend flavours.

Just before serving, stir in mayonnaise.

Makes 6 servings.

▼ ▼ ▼ ▼ ▼ ▼ ▼ ▼ ▼ ▼ ▼ ▼ ▼ ▼ ▼

PUMPKIN & SQUASH

Like so many other foods that we enjoy today, squash was grown first by native people in the Americas. They planted it between rows of corn and the spreading vines kept the weeds down. Although winter squash and pumpkins differ botanically, they are similar foods and are interchangeable in most recipes. Both are high in vitamin A.

ROASTED SEEDS: prepare the seeds for roasting by washing away the pulp; dry. Toss a teaspoon of oil with each cup of seeds and sprinkle with salt. Roast on a shallow tray or baking sheet at 350°F (180°C) for about 10 minutes.

▲ ▲ ▲ ▲ ▲ ▲ ▲ ▲ ▲ ▲ ▲ ▲ ▲ ▲ ▲

PUMPKIN SOUP

*This soup is a fall favourite. We usually reserve the seeds,
which we wash and dry, and later brush lightly with oil,
sprinkle with salt and toast under the broiler for a snack.
You can also make this soup using squash
instead of pumpkin.*

3 cups chicken stock *750 mL*
1 pumpkin, peeled, seeded and cubed
1 tart apple, peeled, cored and cubed
½ Tbsp olive oil *7 mL*
1 onion, chopped
1 clove garlic, finely minced
1 tsp minced gingerroot *5 mL*
1 tsp ground coriander *5 mL*
dash cayenne
salt and pepper

Heat 1 cup (250 mL) of the chicken stock in large pot
and cook pumpkin and apple until tender, about 20 minutes.

Using potato masher, crush pumpkin and apple, and
slowly stir in remaining stock. Heat thoroughly.

Meanwhile, heat oil in skillet; sauté onion, garlic and ginger in oil. Stir onion mixture, coriander, cayenne, salt and
pepper into pot.

Simmer for 10 minutes.

Makes 1 to 6 servings.

GRANDMA'S POTATO SOUP

This recipe, handed down over four generations to Christine Peets, was shared orally and only recently written down. The original recipe called for the potatoes to be cooked in milk for an hour while the cook constantly stirred them to prevent scalding. The tedium of this process has been replaced with the quicker method of gently boiling the potatoes in chicken stock. Christine says that although cooking in stock may be quicker, she prefers her great-grandmother's traditional method, "because it is more than just a pot of soup that I get at the end. I also get a pot of memories of many family suppers." When not in a traditional mood, Christine adds a pinch each of dill, parsley, tarragon and paprika to the soup pot.

3 Tbsp butter *45 mL*
2 large onions, coarsely chopped
6 large potatoes, peeled and cut into eighths
3 cups chicken stock *750 mL*
salt and pepper
2 large carrots, shredded
1 cup cream or milk *250 mL*

Melt butter in large soup pot over high heat.

Cook onions in butter for 3 to 5 minutes until softened.

Add potatoes and cook for 5 minutes. Pour stock over potatoes and onions. Add a pinch of salt and pepper.

Cook over medium heat 12 to 15 minutes until potatoes are tender.

Mash potatoes and onions with stock until soup is consistency of a chowder (the potatoes should still be chunky).

Stir in shredded carrots and adjust seasoning.

Stir in milk and heat to serving temperature.

Makes 4 servings.

▼ ▼ ▼ ▼ ▼ ▼ ▼ ▼ ▼ ▼ ▼ ▼ ▼ ▼ ▼

POTATOES

Potatoes, like so many other foods we enjoy, are rooted in the Americas. In Peru, for example, many different kinds are grown and some of the early stocks, including blue varieties, are once again being tended on a larger scale. Following their conquest of South America, the Spaniards returned to Europe with the wonderful tubers, which are attributed with having saved many Europeans from starvation. Later, however, during the infamous Irish potato famine, many fled their homeland when the potato crop failed. Today's potatoes have been developed for modern tastes and two types dominate the marketplace — the long narrow type used for baking and the rounder type used for boiling. Specialty varieties are also readily available such as the golden-fleshed potatoes that make delicious potato salad. Potatoes provide our bodies with complex carbohydrates and fibre, and if we omit sour cream and dollops of butter, are low in calories.

▲ ▲ ▲ ▲ ▲ ▲ ▲ ▲ ▲ ▲ ▲ ▲ ▲ ▲ ▲ ▲

GARDENER'S RATATOUILLE

*Depending on the season and the garden, ratatouille
ingredients may change, but it remains a vegetable lover's
favourite. When served hot, accompany with garlic
bread; when cold, it's delicious with crusty rolls or rye
and caraway bread.*

2 Tbsp olive oil *25 mL*
2 onions, finely chopped
1 sweet green pepper, diced
1 sweet red pepper, diced
6 cloves garlic, minced
2 stalks celery, chopped
1 cup halved mushrooms *250 mL*
2 cups chopped plum tomatoes *500 mL*
2½ cups corn, cubed eggplant or cubed zucchini *625 mL*
½ tsp oregano *2 mL*
¼ cup chopped fresh parsley *50 mL*
1 Tbsp fresh chopped basil *15 mL*
1 tsp salt *5 mL*
freshly grated black pepper
1 cup shredded mozzarella cheese *250 mL*

Heat oil in large saucepan. Add onions, green and red
peppers and garlic.

Cook over low heat until onions are softened.

Stir in celery, mushrooms, tomatoes, onion mixture, corn
and seasonings.

Cook, covered, over medium heat 30 minutes.

Serve warm or chilled. Top each bowl with pepper and grated mozzarella.

Makes 6 servings.

▼ ▼ ▼ ▼ ▼ ▼ ▼ ▼ ▼ ▼ ▼ ▼ ▼ ▼ ▼

GARLIC BREAD

Slice a French stick on the diagonal (about ½ inch slices), without cutting quite through the bottom of the loaf. Crush 2 cloves garlic; add to ¼ cup butter; spread on bread slices. Wrap loosely in foil. Bake at 350°F for 20 minutes. Serve on a breadboard or in a basket.

▲ ▲ ▲ ▲ ▲ ▲ ▲ ▲ ▲ ▲ ▲ ▲ ▲ ▲ ▲

CORN & POTATO CHOWDER

A meal by itself, this chowder is especially good with
Bannock *(see recipe page 196) warm from the oven.*

6 cups water *1.5 L*
6 potatoes, peeled and cubed
1 onion, chopped
1 stalk celery, chopped
2 cloves garlic, minced
2 vegetable bouillon cubes
dash dried sage
½ tsp dried thyme *2 mL*
½ tsp dried oregano *2 mL*
½ tsp seasoned salt *2 mL*
freshly grated pepper
1 tsp cumin seeds *5 mL*
¼ tsp nutmeg *1 mL*
4 cups corn *1 L*
1 Tbsp butter *15 mL*
¼ cup diced sweet green pepper *50 mL*
½ cup sliced green onions or scallions *125 mL*
1 Tbsp minced fresh dill *15 mL*

Bring water to boil in large pot. Add potatoes, onion,
celery and garlic. Return to boil; add bouillon cubes and
seasonings.

Cover and simmer over medium heat for 15 to 20 minutes, until potatoes are tender.

Remove 2 cups (500 mL) of potatoes and set aside.

Reduce heat to low and add corn. Simmer, stirring to make sure chowder doesn't stick, for 5 minutes.

Meanwhile, melt butter in small skillet. Sauté green pepper and green onions for 3 minutes. Stir into chowder.

Mash reserved potatoes. Return to chowder.

Stir in dill. Adjust seasonings.

Makes 4 generous servings.

Sautéed Garden
Vegetables

Fast, easy and nutritious, this recipe works with almost any combination of vegetables. Since gardens provide an ever changing abundance of produce, substitute what you have on hand for the herbs and vegetables listed. To make a complete meal, serve with pasta that has been tossed with melted butter or olive oil and topped with grated cheese.

3 Tbsp olive oil *45 mL*
2 Tbsp grated fresh gingerroot *25 mL*
1 onion, chopped
½ sweet red or green pepper, diced
1 bunch broccoli, chopped
1 small zucchini, julienned
3 carrots, julienned
1 cup snow peas, topped *250 mL*
1 cup bean sprouts *250 mL*
¼ cup water *50 mL*
½ tsp dried oregano *2 mL*
2 Tbsp chopped fresh basil *25 mL*
salt and pepper

Heat oil in large, heavy skillet or wok; sauté gingerroot for 1 minute. Add vegetables and sauté for 3 minutes or until vegetables are tender-crisp. Add water and partially cover skillet. Steam until fork-tender. Stir in herbs, salt and pepper.

Makes 4 servings.

▼ ▼ ▼ ▼ ▼ ▼ ▼ ▼ ▼ ▼ ▼ ▼ ▼ ▼ ▼

WILD RICE

Wild rice adds a nutty flavour and chewy texture to recipes. Actually, it's not a rice at all,
but rather an aquatic grass that grows naturally in shallow shore waters in Ontario, eastern
Manitoba and Minnesota. Each fall, the grains
are harvested, roasted, hulled and cleaned. To
cook wild rice, stir ½ cup into 1½ cups boiling
water. Simmer 25 to 35 minutes until tender.
Drain.

▲ ▲ ▲ ▲ ▲ ▲ ▲ ▲ ▲ ▲ ▲ ▲ ▲ ▲ ▲

WILD RICE STIR-FRY

Stir-fry cooking at our house depends on what is growing in the garden. We may include snow peas in the spring, green beans in the summer or tomatoes in the fall. Add herbs such as dill and basil, when in season.

3 Tbsp olive oil *45 mL*
1 clove garlic, quartered
12 oz steak (rib-eye, sirloin), sliced thinly crosswise *375 g*
¾ cup sliced mushrooms *175 mL*
1 tomato, peeled and chopped
½ sweet red pepper, diced
4 green onions, sliced
1 tsp grated gingerroot *5 mL*
½ cucumber, seeded and sliced
2 Tbsp soya sauce *25 mL*
freshly grated pepper
1 cup cooked wild rice *250 mL*

Heat oil in heavy skillet or wok. Sauté garlic 5 minutes; discard.

Cook steak strips, mushrooms, tomato, red pepper, green onions and ginger 8 to 10 minutes until steak is browned and vegetables are tender-crisp.

Stir in cucumber, soya sauce and pepper. Add wild rice to skillet. Stir to heat thoroughly. Serve immediately.

Makes 2 servings.

HOT & SPICY BEAN SOUP

This soup requires some forethought (remembering to soak the beans the night before) and some simmering time, but actual time in the kitchen is minimal. When I make this recipe, we usually eat half, and I freeze the remainder for a day that I'm too busy to cook.

4 *cups* navy beans *1 L*
2 *Tbsp* olive oil *25 mL*
2 large, meaty pork hocks
1 large onion, diced
4 cloves garlic, minced
8 *cups* water *2 L*
3 bay leaves
1 *Tbsp* salt *15 mL*
1 *Tbsp* hot pepper flakes *15 mL*
4-6 generous dashes hot sauce
1½ *tsp* dry mustard *7 mL*
¾ *tsp* summer savory *4 mL*
¼ *tsp* pepper *1 mL*
4 *cups* chopped tomatoes *1 L*

Soak beans overnight. Drain and rinse.

Heat oil in large stockpot over high heat; brown pork hocks. Sauté onion and garlic until soft but not browned, 3 or 4 minutes. Stir in beans, water and spices; simmer 2 hours. Add tomatoes and simmer another hour. Taste and adjust seasoning.

Makes 8 servings

MEXICAN REFRIED BEANS

This Mexican staple can be served in corn tortillas or as an accompaniment to tortilla chips. Serve it with bowls of cut lettuce, chopped tomatoes, sour cream or yogurt, avocado slices, grated jack cheese and spicy salsa and let your family members build their own meal.

3 Tbsp oil *45 mL*
1 onion, chopped
½ sweet green pepper, chopped
3 cloves garlic, minced
4 cups cooked kidney, pinto or black beans *1 L*

Heat oil in skillet over medium heat; sauté onion, green pepper and garlic until soft.

Stir in beans and mash roughly in skillet.

Cook uncovered to dry out the beans, about 15 minutes.

Makes 6 servings.

SALSA

Salsa is a flavourful condiment for refried beans and tortillas. Although commercial ones abound, it's a pleasure to make your own when fresh tomatoes are in season.

4 large ripe tomatoes
4 green onions, thinly sliced
3 cloves garlic, minced
3 Tbsp chopped fresh coriander (optional) *45 mL*
2 Tbsp vegetable oil *25 mL*
2 Tbsp vinegar *25 mL*
1 Tbsp finely chopped jalapeño peppers *15 mL*
1 tsp sugar *5 mL*
¼ tsp salt *1 mL*

Cover tomatoes in deep bowl with boiling water for about 2 minutes to make them easy to peel.

Peel, seed and finely chop tomatoes. Place in bowl and stir in remaining ingredients.

Let stand at room temperature 30 minutes for flavours to blend.

Store in refrigerator. Keeps one week.

Makes 4 cups (1 L).

DHAL

Serve this puréed lentil dish with rice and chapatis for a meal of complete protein. Dhal can also be thinned with water and served as a soup, garnished with sautéed onions. Brown lentils are grown on the Prairies while red lentils usually come from the Middle East. Both are an excellent source of vegetable protein.

1 *cup* dried lentils *250 mL*
1½ *Tbsp* vegetable oil *20 mL*
1 large onion, chopped
2 cloves garlic, minced
1 *tsp* grated gingerroot *5 mL*
½ *tsp* turmeric *2 mL*
3 *cups* hot water *750 mL*
½ *tsp* Garam Masala *2 mL*
(see recipe on page 165)
salt

Soak lentils in water for 1 hour; rinse and drain.

Heat oil in skillet over medium heat; sauté onion, garlic and ginger until onions are golden brown. Stir in turmeric until well mixed. Stir in lentils and cook for 2 minutes. Add hot water, return to the boil, reduce heat to simmer and cook, covered, for 20 minutes. Stir in *Garam Masala* and salt to taste and continue cooking, covered, until lentils are soft, about 10 minutes. Remove lid and cook until thick, about 5 minutes.

Makes 4 servings.

CHANNA

*This speedy African/Asian vegetable dish can be served as
a side dish or tucked inside a chapati, a light, flaky flat
bread that soaks up sauce. Chapatis can be purchased in
Indian grocery stores or made from scratch.*
(See recipe on page 209)

2 *Tbsp* vegetable oil *25 mL*
1 sweet green pepper, diced
4 *cups* cooked chick peas, drained *1 L*
2 green onions, finely chopped
1 *tsp* ground cumin *5 mL*
½ *tsp* cayenne pepper (optional) *2 mL*
salt

Heat oil in skillet over medium heat.
Sauté green pepper for 4 minutes.
Stir in chick peas; cook 5 minutes.
Stir in green onions and spices and cook for 10 minutes.

Makes 4 to 6 servings.

OLD CHEDDAR & GARLIC PASTA

Always a hit, this pasta dinner is quick, easy and delicious. A green leafy salad garnished with capers makes a perfect complement to this rich entrée. If you can, purchase cheese that has been naturally aged — it'll be full of flavour and aroma, carrying this dish into the realm of superlatives.

8 oz pasta (rotini or other pasta) *250 g*
½ cup milk or light cream *125 mL*
2 Tbsp butter *25 mL*
4 cloves garlic (peeled but whole)
2 cups grated old white Cheddar cheese (loosely packed) *500 mL*
pepper

Cook pasta in large pot of boiling water for 8 to 10 minutes or until tender but firm.

Meanwhile, in heavy pan, heat milk and butter. Pierce garlic cloves with sharp knife and add to milk mixture; simmer for 5 minutes.

With slotted spoon, remove garlic and discard. Add grated cheese; cook, stirring, over low heat until cheese has melted. Remove from heat and cover.

Drain pasta and toss with sauce; grate pepper over top.

BEEF IT UP:

Thinly slice a small steak crosswise. Sauté in very hot olive oil for 3 to 4 minutes. Add generous dashes of hot sauce and ¼ cup (50 mL) slivered sweet red peppers; sprinkle with salt and pepper. Serve beside pasta.

Makes 2 servings.

▼ ▼ ▼ ▼ ▼ ▼ ▼ ▼ ▼ ▼ ▼ ▼ ▼ ▼

PASTA

Pasta, found in most of the world's cuisines, is high in complex carbohydrates and low in sodium and fat. Canada is known on the world market as a superior grower of durum wheat for pasta. By volume, pasta has fewer calories than either potatoes or rice. It is made by combining ground grain (wheat, buckwheat, rice or spelt) with water. Pasta is simple to prepare, nutritious, delicious and a perfect companion to *Sautéed Garden Vegetables* (see recipe on page 130). Fresh pasta is perfect served immediately and dressed with a light sauce. However, for marinated salads, dried pastas holds up better. A rule of thumb is to cook 4 oz (100 g) for each person. For every 4 oz (100 g) of pasta use 4 cups (1 L) of boiling water. It is important that the water not stop boiling when the pasta is added. Fresh pasta cooks in a couple of minutes; dried pasta may need 8 to 10.

▲ ▲ ▲ ▲ ▲ ▲ ▲ ▲ ▲ ▲ ▲ ▲ ▲ ▲

DIJON FILLETS

Fish is the quintessential fast food. For this recipe, use almost any fillets — sole, perch or salmon. Serve with rice, a steamed vegetable and Garden Salad with Basil Vinaigrette *(see recipe page 82).*

½ Tbsp butter *7 mL*
2 fish fillets
⅓ cup white wine *75 mL*
1 Tbsp Dijon mustard *15 mL*
1 tsp capers *5 mL*

Melt butter in heavy skillet over medium heat.

Add fish fillets and cook 3 to 6 minutes on each side, depending on thickness, or until fillets flake when pierced with fork.

Remove from pan and keep warm.

Stir wine, mustard and capers into skillet and cook, stirring at high heat, until liquid is reduced by half.

Pour over fillets and serve.

Makes 2 servings.

PASTA WITH
MEDITERRANEAN FLAVOURS

This is the ideal dish to serve to friends who announce they're vegetarian and have also given up eating eggs, milk and dairy products. Put on opera music and start chopping. Try to be consistent so that the carrot pieces are cut the same size. Then move on to the next vegetable and make it slightly different. Consistency of cut size gives recipes a professional look. You can leave out any of the vegetables except the garlic, capers and black olives.

3 Tbsp olive oil *45 mL*

1 onion, diced

4 cloves garlic, minced

2 carrots, diced

2 stalks celery, diced

6 mushrooms, sliced

1 sweet green pepper, diced

¼ cup chopped, pitted black olives *50 mL*

¼ cup chopped, pitted green olives (optional) *50 mL*

½ jar (6 oz/175 mL) artichoke hearts (optional)

2 Tbsp capers *25 mL*

4 cups canned plum tomatoes *1 L*

1 lb pasta *500 g*

Heat oil in large skillet over medium heat.

Add onion and garlic and cook, stirring occasionally until softened.

Stir in carrots, celery, mushrooms, green pepper, olives and artichoke hearts.

Cook on low heat for 5 minutes.

Stir in capers and tomatoes. Simmer until sauce is thick, about 20 minutes.

Meanwhile cook pasta in large pot of boiling salted water for 10 minutes or until tender but firm. Drain.

Mix sauce and pasta and serve in bowl.

Makes 4 servings.

PASTA WITH SPICY LAMB SAUCE

Although it's easy to buy frozen New Zealand lamb, I always look for fresh local lamb. Lamb can graze on marginal land and are still raised outside in the elements. This recipe uses shoulder or loin chops.

1 lb lamb *500 g*
4 Tbsp olive oil *60 mL*
1 small onion, diced
3 cloves garlic, minced
1½ tsp dried rosemary *7 mL*
½ tsp red pepper flakes *2 mL*
1 cup red wine, stock or water *250 mL*
4 cups canned tomatoes or homemade tomato sauce *1 L*
salt
1 lb penne or other pasta *500 g*
3 Tbsp chopped fresh parsley *45 mL*
4 Tbsp grated Parmesan cheese *60 mL*

Remove fat from lamb. Cut meat into bean-sized slivers.

Heat oil in heavy skillet over medium heat. Stir in onion, garlic, rosemary and red pepper flakes and cook until onion is soft.

Stir in lamb slivers and cook until no longer pink.

Raise heat to high, stir in wine and cook 2 minutes until liquid is reduced.

Stir in tomatoes and salt to taste. Cover and cook on low heat for 45 minutes.

Meanwhile cook pasta in large pot of boiling salted water for 10 minutes or until tender but firm. Drain.

Stir into lamb sauce. Turn into a serving bowl. Top with parsley and cheese.

Makes 4 servings.

CHICKEN BREASTS

For a fast and easy dinner, set brown rice on the stove to cook. Prepare the chicken breasts, and while they are simmering, wash greens for a leafy salad and make Lemon Dressing *(see recipe page 88). In very little time, you have a dinner to share with friends.*

4 chicken breasts
flour
salt and pepper
3 Tbsp olive oil *45 mL*
½ cup chopped tomatoes *125 mL*
½ cup sliced mushrooms *125 mL*
½ cup chopped green onions *50 mL*
¼ cup white wine *50 mL*

Dredge chicken breasts in flour, salt and pepper.

In heavy skillet, heat oil; brown chicken breasts for 4 minutes on each side.

Stir in remaining ingredients, cover and simmer for 20 minutes until tender.

Makes 4 servings.

CHICKEN SOUP WITH DUMPLINGS

This recipe comes from Pearlyn Baptiste, who helped set up and run a Saturday morning fruit and vegetable market in her community. Pearlyn also caters festivals and musical events and is about to open her own restaurant. In Grenada, where she comes from, soup is thought to cure everything from depression to colds.

6 to 8 pieces chicken (white or dark meat)
¼ cup white vinegar 50 mL
½ onion, diced
1 clove garlic, crushed
salt
2 large carrots
2 celery stalks
2 potatoes
½ cup flour 125 mL
1 tsp sugar 5 mL
1 tsp butter 5 mL
2 Tbsp warm water 30 mL
12 spaghetti noodles
1 tsp black pepper 5 mL
1 sprig thyme

Remove skin from chicken. Cut chicken into bite-sized pieces. Wash chicken with vinegar; rinse with cold water to cut grease. Sprinkle onion, garlic and salt over chicken pieces.

Bring 8 cups (2 L) water to boil in large soup pot. Add chicken mixture and boil gently. Meanwhile, peel and slice carrots, slice celery, and peel and cube potatoes. Add carrots, celery and potatoes to pot.

Mix flour, sugar, butter and warm water in small bowl to form ball that doesn't stick.

Roll out dough on floured surface and get the kids to help you form about 8 dumplings.

Drop dumplings into soup; break noodles into quarters and add to soup. Cook 10 minutes. Add salt to taste, pepper and thyme.

Makes 8 to 10 servings.

SATAY

Satay, an Indonesian treat of grilled meat on skewers, is often served there by street vendors. Peanut Sauce, bas-mati rice and a salad complete the meal at home. All the preparation is done ahead and at the last minute, the skewers are barbequed or placed on a baking sheet and grilled in the oven.

1 lb sirloin beef, chicken or pork *500 g*

MARINADE

1 tsp grated lemon rind *5 mL*

2 onions

1 Tbsp soya sauce *15 mL*

1 Tbsp vegetable oil *15 mL*

2 tsp ground coriander *10 mL*

1 tsp ground cumin *5 mL*

1 tsp turmeric *5 mL*

¼ tsp cinnamon *1 mL*

1 tsp salt *5 mL*

1 tsp sugar *5 mL*

⅓ cup water *75 mL*

Cut meat into small cubes the size of your fingertip.

Blend marinade ingredients in blender or food processor. Pour over cubes of meat, cover and marinate in refrigerator for 1 hour or longer.

Meanwhile soak small bamboo skewers in water for 1 hour to prevent them from burning during cooking.

Thread meat cubes so that they're barely touching onto wet skewers and barbeque or grill for five minutes on each side or until done.

Makes 4 servings.

PEANUT SAUCE

*Peanut sauce can be purchased or made and stored in the
refrigerator for up to a week. Serve the sauce with
Satay and rice.*

1 cup coconut milk (see recipe on page 41) *250 mL*
½ cup peanut butter *125 mL*
2 cloves garlic, minced
2 tsp brown sugar *10 mL*
4 Tbsp soya sauce or tamari *60 mL*
3 Tbsp lemon juice *45 mL*
½ tsp red pepper flakes (optional) *2 mL*
salt

Stir coconut milk and peanut butter together in saucepan
and cook over low heat until mixed.

Remove from heat and stir in remaining ingredients,
adding water if necessary to thin it.

Makes 1 cup (250 mL).

CHICKEN WITH LEMON & CAPERS

This elegant dish takes just a few minutes. You can sub-
stitute veal, pork cutlets or sliced turkey breast for the
chicken. Do not use an aluminum pan as the capers and
lemon will react to turn the dish blue-green.

2 Tbsp   olive oil   *25 mL*
1 Tbsp   butter   *15 mL*
3 cloves garlic, minced
4 boneless chicken portions or chicken breasts
½ cup   white wine or lemon juice   *125 mL*
2 Tbsp   capers   *25 mL*
½ cup   water   *125 mL*
4 Tbsp   chopped fresh parsley   *60 mL*

Heat oil and butter in skillet until foaming. Add garlic
and stir. (Don't let it brown). Add chicken and cook 3 minutes on each side. Stir in wine and capers. Then add water.

Cover, lower heat to simmer and cook for 10 minutes
until chicken is no longer pink. Remove lid and turn up heat
to reduce the sauce to a spoonful for each portion.

Sprinkle with chopped parsley and serve.

Makes 4 servings.

▼ ▼ ▼ ▼ ▼ ▼ ▼ ▼ ▼ ▼ ▼ ▼ ▼ ▼ ▼

CAPERS

Capers are the green buds of a plant that
grows wild around the Mediterranean. They
are pickled and give a sharp, spicy sour taste
to a recipe. Look for tiny jars at specialty
food stores.

▲ ▲ ▲ ▲ ▲ ▲ ▲ ▲ ▲ ▲ ▲ ▲ ▲ ▲ ▲

Leek & Potato Frittata

A frittata is an open-faced omelette. Instead of leeks, you can substitute corn cut from the cob and slivers of red pepper or onions that have been cooked until light brown and sprinkled with a few drops of balsamic vinegar. Use a skillet that can go under the broiler.

2 red potatoes, halved
2 leeks, cut in half lengthwise
3 Tbsp butter *45 mL*
7 eggs
¾ tsp dried marjoram *4 mL*
pinch nutmeg
salt and pepper
½ cup grated Cheddar or hard cheese *125 mL*
¼ cup chopped fresh parsley *50 mL*

Cook potatoes in boiling water until just tender, about 15 minutes. Drain, cool and slice thinly.

Using only white and light green part of leeks, slice thinly crosswise. Melt butter in skillet over medium heat until foaming. Add leeks, stirring frequently, and cook 5 minutes. Stir in sliced potatoes gently to mix; cook about 5 minutes.

Preheat broiler. Beat eggs, marjoram, nutmeg, salt and pepper to taste in bowl. Pour over potato-leek mixture. Cover and cook on low heat until eggs are set, about 10 minutes.

Sprinkle with cheese. Put skillet under broiler until cheese melts and browns, about 3 to 5 minutes. Sprinkle with parsley. Cut in wedges and serve.

Makes 4 servings.

ROOTS & SUNSHINE VEGETABLES

THE BIKE RIDE:
ABUNDANCE AND VARIETY

FROM THE END OF APRIL, till the beginning of October, I usually ride my bike with its huge canvas saddlebags five miles downtown to work at Field to Table. I concentrate on just getting there most mornings, but the real joy is the ride home.

If I go one route, I often stop at a small Mom and Pop Portuguese kitchen. Their specialties are marinated black olives and chicken that's split, marinated in herb-scented oil and then barbequed over coals. The cook spritzes the chicken with water occasionally and there's no hurrying the process. If you're too early, you can sit and have an expresso at the café next door and watch the passing parade or you can go to the bakery on the other side of the café and pick up little yellow custard tarts, slightly caramelized atop flaky pastry, and small loaves of dense cornbread. Once home, a salad takes only five minutes.

Other evenings, I go through Chinatown and buy the first lichee nuts of the season and yard-long beans. If I'm lucky, the bakery will have the sticky translucent rice cakes that my daughter loves. With each visit I get more adventuresome: fresh fat hollow noodles for soups, coconut milk, green tea and tamarind paste.

Another route home along King Street offers Caribbean food. A queenly woman presides in a spotless café and serves up freshly made roti with your choice of vegetarian or meat fillings: channa, potatoes, mutton, goat, chicken or beef. Then she asks "hot sauce?" and believe me, a few drops will do.

I take my time pedalling home, enjoying the best of a big city, with its never-ending variety of people, culture and food.

M.L.M.

ROOTS AND SUNSHINE VEGETABLES

WORKING WITH DIFFERENT immigrant and cultural groups through Field to Table has given me a new understanding of how we all see food differently. As an example, many Jamaican customers laughed uproariously at the small zucchini and eggplant I bought for them. Perhaps because of the lushness and the quick growing season in the tropics everything has the potential to grow large and these customers associate size with ripeness. On the other hand, Canadian customers complain about large cabbages and zucchinis, equating small ones with good quality.

Recently, immigrants from Bosnia refused to buy oranges and lemons, even though the prices were reasonable. In their experience, these items are usually available only at Christmas. With many of their relatives living in wartime conditions in Bosnia, this daily luxury of abundant fresh fruit was too great a contrast.

It is easy to make assumptions. We respect the restrictions of Muslims and Jews against pork but it was only recently through our customers that I learned about the dietary restrictions of the Jains. The Jains, an East Indian religious community, do not drink alcohol or eat meat, honey or many seed-filled vegetables. They believe that food is sacred, and that all living beings possess souls. Some 32 vegetables, primarily root ones, are thought to house not one but many souls and eating them is forbidden.

The richness of our country is demonstrated in the diversity of our traditions and our easy access to almost unlimited varieties of food. New cultures will continue to influence what is grown, brought to market and cooked in our homes. Ten years ago snow peas, eggplant, bok choy, basil and even coriander were not readily available in Canada unless you grew your own. Today, Canadian farmers grow these items, which are commonly found in almost every supermarket along with imported plantains, kiwifruit and Granny Smith apples.

In turn, new Canadians will become spoiled as they realize that the cost of our food is the second lowest in the world. Only the Americans have cheaper food. Immigrants will venture to cook such typically North American vegetables as asparagus, beet tops, parsnips and turnips, using their own spicing and cooking techniques. They will come to appreciate how short our growing season is and how the seasons influence the kind of food our bodies need. The fall harvest brings a glut of choice. But after that first frost, the food supply changes. Corn stops growing in the field. The leaves of the squash plant shrivel, exposing the fruit. The skins of tomatoes and peppers are damaged beyond salvaging.

After the fall, more food is imported, with prices escalating during the holidays. Our farmers have perfected the process of storing apples, pears and root vegetables; these always seem to be reasonably priced and well suited to the harsh winter, which calls for a heavy, robust and comforting diet.

The end of winter signals a time for different clothes and different foods. We crave cleansing herbs, raw food and light green salads. Summer is pure indulgence with wild and commercially produced berries, tender fruit, new onions and potatoes and many greens. Locally grown fragile lettuces, which don't travel well across continents, can be harvested and sold the next day.

Many people change their buying habits in the summer and seek out farmers markets and roadside stands. City people venture miles out of town to pick their own fruits and vegetables and are surprised to find out how hot and hard the work is. And then they have to freeze or can any excess.

Another way to bridge the gap between farmers and city people, which is catching on across North America, is called Community Shared Agriculture. Families purchase shares in a market garden and agree to pay in advance for their portion of the harvest. In this way, they share in the risks and rewards of farming. Their farmer, in turn, will negotiate with the sharers about what to grow and how to grow it.

In 1994 in Toronto, 250 families agreed to pay $225 each for a share in the harvest of the Colectivo Agricola Latino. The farmers are a group of El Salvadorean immigrants who rented 45 acres of land near Beaverton and are farming organically. On Wednesday, they pick the vegetables and on Thursdays they deliver 250 nearly identical baskets of food to 14 neighbourhood drop-off points throughout the city.

The city families who are customers of the collective learn about the seasonality of food and some of the problems farmers face and come to appreciate the rain, even on weekends. The farmers receive retail prices for their food, are assured of their market and learn more about the customer's way of thinking.

From $480,000 in 1991 to $6 million in 1993, Community Shared Agriculture ventures in Canada and the United States are growing quickly. They're a mere drop in the bucket of total agricultural sales but they're helping bridge the gap between farming and eating.

M.L.M

GOBHI MASALA
(SPICED CAULIFLOWER)

Georgia Nayyar came to Canada from Greece when she was 10 years old. She remembers life on the farm there and going with her father to get water for the fields. In Canada she married into an Indian family and, through patience and observation, has become an excellent cook of Indian dishes.

2 *Tbsp* vegetable oil *25 mL*
2 *tsp* mustard seeds *10 mL*
4 *tsp* chopped peeled gingerroot *20 mL*
1 large cauliflower
¼ *tsp* turmeric *1 mL*
½ *tsp* cumin seeds *2 mL*
¼ *tsp* poppy seeds *1 mL*
2 pods black cardamom, crushed
salt
3 *tsp* chopped fresh coriander *15 mL*

Heat a mild-flavoured vegetable oil (not olive oil) in skillet over medium-high heat. Add mustard seeds. When they snap and pop, add chopped gingerroot and sauté for 2 to 3 minutes.

Meanwhile, cut cauliflower into florets.

Stir in cauliflower, turmeric, cumin seeds, poppy seeds,

crushed cardamom and salt to taste.

Stir until cauliflower turns yellow. Sprinkle with 1 Tbsp (15 mL) water.

Cover and cook on high for 1 minute to build up steam. Then turn heat down, uncover and simmer 15 minutes. This allows steam to escape so cauliflower is dry.

Sprinkle with fresh coriander.

Makes 6 to 8 servings.

▼ ▼ ▼ ▼ ▼ ▼ ▼ ▼ ▼ ▼ ▼ ▼ ▼ ▼ ▼

CORIANDER

Coriander, cilantro, or Chinese parsley, is a
fresh herb that looks like parsley but
has its own unique peppery flavour. It's often
used in Indian and Spanish cooking.
Parsley can be substituted.

▲ ▲ ▲ ▲ ▲ ▲ ▲ ▲ ▲ ▲ ▲ ▲ ▲ ▲ ▲

EGGPLANT & POTATOES

This is another cross-cultural recipe from Georgia Nayyar. In recognition of many wonderful shared meals, Georgia's friends have put together a book of her Indian recipes called Cooking with Georgia.

4 large potatoes
1 large eggplant
4 Tbsp vegetable oil *60 mL*
1 onion, chopped
4 cloves garlic, chopped
1 Tbsp chopped peeled gingerroot *15 mL*
1 tsp cumin seeds *5 mL*
1 tsp ground coriander *5 mL*
½ tsp turmeric *2 mL*
2 fresh tomatoes, chopped
salt
1 tsp Garam Masala *5 mL*

Peel potatoes. Leave skin on eggplant for colour. Cut eggplant and potatoes into ½ inch (1 cm) cubes.

Heat oil in deep pan over medium heat. Add onion, garlic and ginger. Stir and cook until brown, about 5 minutes.

Stir in cumin seeds, ground coriander and turmeric and cook for 1 minute.

Stir in tomatoes and continue cooking for 5 minutes.

Stir in potatoes, eggplant, salt and ½ cup (125 mL) water.

Cover and cook on low heat about 20 minutes, stirring occasionally. Sprinkle with *Garam Masala* just before serving.

Makes 6 to 8 servings.

GARAM MASALA

2 Tbsp black cardamom seeds *25 mL*
1 Tbsp black peppercorns *15 mL*
1 tsp ground cloves *5 mL*
1 tsp green cardamom seeds *5 mL*
1 tsp cumin seeds *5 mL*
1 2 inch (5 cm) stick cinnamon

Grind in spice or coffee grinder, may be stored refrigerated in an airtight jar for up to 1 month.

Makes ¼ cup (50 mL).

RAITA

A cooling accompaniment to Indian food, this dish is delicious served with Gobhi Masala, Eggplant and Potatoes *and basmati rice.*

2 cups plain low-fat yogurt *500 mL*
½ English cucumber, grated
salt
fresh black pepper
paprika

Stir together all the ingredients, cover and refrigerate for 1 hour so flavours will blend.

Makes 2 cups (500 mL).

OVEN-ROASTED VEGETABLES

The trick to this recipe is to cut the vegetables in sizes so that they can all go into the oven at once and finish cooking at the same time. For example, the potatoes need to be cut smaller than the zucchini as they cook differently. A little experimenting will reveal the best sizes. The roasting brings out the sweetness of each vegetable. Be sure to cook vegetables in a single layer in a shallow pan so that they roast rather than steam.

2 zucchini, sliced in 1 inch (2.5 cm) rounds
1 eggplant (skin on) cut in 1 inch (2.5 cm) cubes
1 lb green beans, cut in 2 inch (5 cm) lengths *500 g*
3 onions, cut in crescents
3 unpeeled potatoes, cut in wedges
2 green peppers, seeded and cut in chunks
¼ cup olive oil *50 mL*
3 cloves garlic, finely chopped
2 Tbsp coarse salt or 1 tsp (5 mL) fine salt *25 mL*
⅓ cup lemon juice *75 mL*
½ cup chopped fresh parsley or basil *125 mL*

Put cut-up zucchini, eggplant, green beans, onions, potatoes and green peppers into large roasting pan.

Sprinkle with olive oil, garlic and salt. Stir so that oil coats all vegetables.

Bake for 50 to 60 minutes at 400°F (200°C) or until potatoes are done.

Remove from oven. Pour lemon juice over hot vegetables and sprinkle with fresh parsley or basil. Serve hot or cold.

Makes 4 main-course or 6 side-dish servings.

SHREDDED CARROT SALAD

Prepare this salad in the morning for an evening meal, but leftovers are fine refrigerated for a day or two. This salad has no added sugar, yet it tastes surprisingly sweet.

4 cups shredded carrots *1 L*
1 cup raisins *250 mL*
¼ cup vegetable oil *50 mL*
3 Tbsp lemon juice *45 mL*
¼ tsp salt *1 mL*
dash pepper
1 large tomato, chopped
1 cup almonds *250 mL*

Stir carrots, raisins, oil, lemon juice, salt and pepper to taste in bowl.

Cover and marinate in refrigerator for at least 2 hours.

Just before serving, stir in chopped tomato and nuts.

Makes 4 servings.

PEPERONATA

This Italian autumn dish is best made when peppers are harvested just before the frost. It tastes wonderful with an omelette.

⚜

⅓ *cup* olive oil *75 mL*
1 large onion, halved and sliced
4 sweet green peppers, seeded and cut into strips
2 sweet red peppers, seeded and cut into strips
2 large tomatoes, chopped
1 tiny hot red pepper (optional)
salt and pepper

Heat oil in skillet over medium heat and cook onion for 5 minutes.

Add green and red peppers and cook, stirring until softened, about 20 minutes.

Stir in tomatoes and hot red pepper (if using). Cover and simmer for 15 minutes.

Remove lid and increase heat to medium, cooking for about 3 minutes until any liquid reduces.

Salt and pepper to taste. Serve hot or cold.

Makes 4 to 6 servings.

ROASTED POTATOES

Potatoes, squash and tomatoes are native to the Americas.
Meat and potatoes were the mainstay of the diet of
English, Scottish and Irish immigrants. Potatoes store
well through harsh winters, and are an unexpected
source of vitamin C.

2 lb potatoes, peeled and cut into chunks *1 kg*
4 cloves garlic, peeled and crushed
2 Tbsp dried rosemary *25 mL*
¼ cup olive oil *50 mL*
1 cup water *250 mL*
salt and pepper

Put potatoes, garlic, rosemary and olive oil in shallow
baking pan, stirring until potatoes are lightly coated with oil.
Stir in water and cook for 45 minutes to 1 hour at 425°F
(220°C). Salt and pepper to taste.

Makes 4 servings.

SCALLOPED POTATOES

Scalloped potatoes are the original comfort food. The white sauce is a traditional recipe that can be used as a base for macaroni and cheese, or cream soups.

2 lb potatoes, peeled *1 kg*
1 large onion, thinly sliced
salt and pepper
3 Tbsp butter *45 mL*
3 Tbsp flour *45 mL*
2 cups 2% or whole milk *500 mL*

Slice potatoes thinly and layer with onions, salting and peppering each layer, in shallow 8 inch (2 L) casserole.

Melt butter in saucepan over medium heat. Stir in flour and cook for 2 minutes, stirring constantly. Stir in milk and heat, stirring just until tiny bubbles form around sides of pan.

Pour sauce over potatoes and bake for 1 hour at 400°F (200°C). Sauce will thicken as it bakes.

Makes 4 servings.

PURÉED PARSNIPS

Parsnips are a white root vegetable shaped like a carrot.
A touch of frost in the field enhances their flavour.
Parsnips are a Canadian-grown and exported vegetable,
full of vitamin A and minerals. This purée is
delicious with steamed zucchini.

8 parsnips, peeled and sliced into rounds
4 Tbsp whole milk or cream *60 mL*
1 Tbsp butter *15 mL*
salt and pepper

Cook parsnips in top part of a double boiler in boiling water until tender, about 15 minutes. Drain well.

Mash with a potato masher in the pot.

Place pot over bottom of double boiler filled with boiling water. Stir in milk, butter, and salt and pepper to taste and cook for an additional 15 minutes, stirring occasionally. The further cooking and milk bring out a sweetness in the parsnips.

Makes 6 servings.

RUTABAGAS FOR ROYALTY

Rutabagas are the thick bulbous root vegetable that comes coated with wax in the supermarkets. Like parsnips, rutabagas are often thought of as poverty food and are avoided by younger cooks and are unfamiliar to most immigrants. In fact, they are another very Canadian vegetable that helped early settlers survive the long winters. Vitamins A and C as well as potassium, magnesium and other minerals are found in these roots.
The hardest part of preparing this dense vegetable is cutting it up. Five minutes in the microwave on high will make cutting easier.

1 rutabaga, peeled and cubed
1 Tbsp butter *15 mL*
⅔ cup diced onion *150 mL*
1 Tbsp flour *15 mL*
¾ cup vegetable stock or water *175 mL*
¼ tsp sugar *1 mL*
¼ tsp sage *1 mL*
salt and pepper

Cook rutabaga in boiling salted water for 15 minutes. Drain and set aside.

Melt butter in pot and sauté onion until soft but not brown. Blend in flour and cook for 2 minutes on low heat.

Stir in stock, sugar, sage, salt and pepper to taste and rutabaga.

Cover and continue cooking for 30 minutes until rutabaga is tender and sauce is thickened and reduced.

Mash lightly.

Makes 6 servings.

Scandinavian-Style Red Cabbage, Beets & Apples

This winter dish combines vegetables that store well. The sweet-and-sour taste and rich ruby colour satisfy both the tongue and eye.

3 Tbsp vegetable oil *45 mL*
1 large onion, cut in crescents
1 small red cabbage, finely shredded
2 large beets, peeled and grated
2 apples, cored and cut in wedges
3 Tbsp apple cider vinegar *45 mL*
2 Tbsp brown sugar or maple syrup *25 mL*
1 cup water *250 mL*

Heat oil in large skillet over high heat. Sauté onions until soft. Add red cabbage and beets and stir until all vegetables are lightly coated with oil.

Stir in apples, vinegar, sugar and water.

Cover and cook over low heat for about 30 minutes, or until vegetables are soft.

Makes 6 to 8 servings.

GREEN TOMATO
MINCEMEAT

*This is a mild mincemeat — subtle and not too rich. It's
an excellent way of saving the last green tomatoes
from the frost.*

16 cups chopped green tomatoes *4 L*
4 quarts tart apples, peeled, cored and chopped *4 L*
4 cups raisins, chopped *1 L*
4 cups currants, chopped *1 L*
2 oranges, seeded and chopped
1 lemon, seeded and chopped
10 cups sugar *2.5 L*
2½ cups apple cider *625 mL*
1 cup brandy *250 mL*
½ cup lemon juice *125 mL*
1 Tbsp cinnamon *15 mL*
1 Tbsp salt *15 mL*
1 tsp ground cloves *5 mL*

Combine all ingredients in large kettle. Bring to a slow
boil and simmer until thick, 2 to 3 hours.

Ladle into hot sterilized Mason jars, leaving 1 inch (2.5 cm)
headspace.

Cover with lids that have been boiled for 5 minutes.

Tighten lids and then undo one-quarter turn.

Set jars on rack in boiling water bath and process for 30 minutes; remove from water and set on rack. As jars cool, lids will be sucked down, ensuring a vacuum.

Store in a cool dark place. Will keep for 1 year.

Makes 21 jars, each 2 cups (500 mL).

CHILI SAUCE

Making chili sauce is a fall ritual for many people. This recipe is a variation of my grandmother's. Mine is a little hotter, but its roots go directly back to her early memories of the marvellous tomato sauce she first tasted at her grandma's table. Summer suppers on my grandparents' farm were usually simple and quick — everyone was too tired to cook. Home fries and scrambled eggs or perhaps a slice of leftover roast beef were generously dredged in one or another condiment. The tang and piquancy of chutneys, relishes and chili sauce enliven quiet meals.

11 quarts tomatoes, peeled and chopped *11 L*
14 onions, chopped
5 sweet green peppers, coarsely chopped
5 sweet red peppers, coarsely chopped
1 hot pepper, coarsely chopped
2 cups cider vinegar *500 mL*
1 cup packed brown sugar *250 mL*
1½ cups white sugar *375 mL*
6 tsp salt *90 mL*
1½ Tbsp cinnamon *20 mL*
1 Tbsp ground cloves *15 mL*
1½ tsp cayenne *7 mL*
1 tsp black pepper *5 mL*
1 tsp ground ginger *5 mL*
1 tsp nutmeg *5 mL*

Mix all ingredients in large canning kettle.

Simmer until thick, stirring occasionally, about 5 hours.

Ladle into hot sterilized Mason jars, leaving 1 inch (2.5 cm) headspace. Cover with lids that have been boiled for 5 minutes. Tighten lids and then undo one-quarter turn.

Set jars on rack in boiling water bath and process for 30 minutes; remove from water and set on rack. As jars cool, lids will be sucked down, ensuring a vacuum.

Store in a cool, dark place. After about a month, the flavours will mellow and it's ready for serving.

After opening, keep in refrigerator.

Makes 12 jars, each 2 cups (500 mL).

BREAD & BUTTER PICKLES

Surplus cucumbers in August present a challenge for someone who doesn't like to waste food. Corry Martens, a farm woman from Eastern Ontario, shares this easy pickle recipe that brings the garden inside all winter long. The pickles need to sit for six weeks before they're ready to eat.

10 cucumbers, thinly sliced
6 onions, thinly sliced
¼ cup coarse salt *50 mL*
2½ cups white vinegar *625 mL*
2½ cups sugar *625 mL*
4 tsp celery seed *20 mL*
2 tsp mustard seed *10 mL*
1 tsp turmeric *5 mL*

Mix cucumbers, onions and salt together in a glass or pottery bowl. Leave overnight.

Bring vinegar, sugar, celery and mustard seed to boil in large kettle.

Add cucumbers and onions; return to boil, stirring regularly. Boil until cucumber changes colour, about 10 minutes.Remove from heat, and stir in turmeric. Let cool slightly.

Ladle into hot sterilized Mason jars, leaving 1 inch (2.5 cm) headspace. Cover with lids that have been boiled for 5 minutes. Tighten lids and then undo one-quarter turn.

Set jars on rack in boiling water bath and process for 30 minutes; remove from water and set on rack. As jars cool, lids will be sucked down, ensuring a vacuum.

Store in a cool dark place. Will keep for 1 year.

Makes 12 jars, each 2 cups (500 mL).

▼ ▼ ▼ ▼ ▼ ▼ ▼ ▼ ▼ ▼ ▼ ▼ ▼ ▼ ▼

PICKLING HINTS

Select small, firm unwaxed cucumbers and remove blossom and stem end. Use non-iodized salt. Choose a vinegar with 4 to 6% acidity. Avoid copper, tin, galvanized or brass utensils; instead use wooden, plastic or stainless steel. If pickles require soaking in a brine, select glass or a pottery crock.

▲ ▲ ▲ ▲ ▲ ▲ ▲ ▲ ▲ ▲ ▲ ▲ ▲ ▲ ▲

End-of-the-Garden Relish

This recipe was shared by a group of women in the city who decided to do some pickling together — some for the first time, others, for the first time in ages. This particular recipe was contributed by a woman from the Maritimes who remembered her mother making it. When I went to visit there were cases of shiny, neatly labelled jars of sauces and pickles, discussion of relishes from other countries and plans for a shared garden plot for the coming spring. I found it touching that it had retained its original name even though the vegetables came from Field to Table rather than from their own gardens.

10 carrots, sliced
6 cups white vinegar *1.5 L*
5 cups sugar *1.25 L*
1 cup flour *250 mL*
½ cup dry mustard *125 mL*
2 tsp turmeric *10 mL*
1 tsp celery seed *5 mL*
1 cauliflower, cut into small florets
1 sweet red pepper, seeded and diced
3 onions, diced
2 cucumbers, diced
1 stalk celery, diced

Cook carrots in boiling water for 15 minutes.

Mix together sugar, flour, mustard, vinegar, turmeric and celery seed in large pot.

Add vegetables, cover and cook over medium-high heat for 5 minutes, stirring occasionally.

Ladle into hot sterilized Mason jars, leaving 1 inch (2.5 cm) headspace. Cover with lids that have been boiled for 5 minutes. Tighten lids and then undo one-quarter turn.

Set jars on rack in boiling water bath and process for 30 minutes; remove from water and set on rack. As jars cool, lids will be sucked down, ensuring a vacuum. Store in a cool dark place. Will keep for 1 year.

Makes 10 pints (5 L).

BREADS &
GRAINS

EATING IS AN AGRICULTURAL ACT: HOW THE FOOD SYSTEM WORKS

HOW THE FOOD SYSTEM WORKS is a bit of a mystery but it's all based on making money. Everyone in the chain — the farmer, packer, broker, wholesaler, trucker and retailer — needs a share. How much of the share they get and who controls the price are the real issues.

The food system is further complicated by the fact that there are really only a few buyers, the chainstore retailers. And this is where the power resides in our food system. However, farmers aren't totally powerless. Just as teachers, lawyers and taxi drivers have organized into unions, associations and co-operatives, so have growers. In Canada, after many years of instability during the 1930s to 1950s, farmers of some commodities organized into compulsory co-operatives. This is called a supply-managed system. In a clear example of grass-roots democracy in action, they created our current system.

Now we have marketing boards for eggs, chicken, dairy products, apples, greenhouse vegetables — 25 different organizations in Ontario in all. Their powers vary. Some boards negotiate prices, control how much can be produced and jointly fund research and advertising. The larger boards hire managers to run the day-to-day operations. Smaller boards such as the Asparagus Grower's Marketing Board and the Sheep Marketing Agency Board are run by elected members who volunteer their own time. Each farm has a vote to elect local committee members, who in turn, elect a board of directors. If the majority of farmers don't like the policy directions set, the board gets voted out.

Many consumers and media believe that marketing boards are responsible for the fact that our food prices are higher than those in the United States. Some people think that the General Agreement on Tariffs and Trade (GATT) means that marketing boards will eventually be phased out. The truth is that marketing boards are changing, but they'll continue to represent farmers. I think that if marketing boards did not exist, we'd need to invent them — or associations like them — simply because farmers need a collective voice.

As near as I can figure, when it comes to produce, the farmer gets about one third to one quarter of the final retail price. With processed food, farmers usually get much less of the final retail price. You may have heard the famous example that the cardboard box cookies come in costs more than the wheat in the whole box of cookies. In fact, in 1990 the average Canadian wheat grower received 4 cents for the wheat in a box of cookies, which is down 2 cents from 1980. But the average retail price of the cookies has increased 132 percent over the same time period. Given trends like these, it's difficult to blame farmers and marketing boards for rising food prices.

The Farm Products Marketing Commission, which both Kathryn and I sit on, oversees all 25 marketing boards and associations in Ontario. We're part of a 12-person commission made up of producers, processors, retailers, food-service people and consumers, appointed to oversee the public interest. Every province has a similar commission to oversee its marketing boards.

Sitting on the Commission has been an invaluable learning experience. After 25 years working at the wholesale and retail level of the food business in the city, I have an opportunity to see the big agricultural picture. At the Commission we're briefed on the pressures of globalization and free trade on our agricultural sector. Among other issues last year we discussed the GATT talks, falling trade barriers and the future of biotechnology on the farm. Like so much of our economy, agriculture is in a whirlwind of change and restructuring.

Kathryn and I have a lot of the same doubts and questions about our food system. We see how farmers and consumers are separated by the food distribution system and pitted against each other.

I have heard farmers describe the typical consumer as someone who cares only for the lowest possible price, someone willing to drive 30 miles to the border for a 10-cent-a-litre difference in the price of milk. Although some consumers are price-driven, I think many are also interested in other issues, such as better nutrition, good taste and accurate labelling information. As an example, some consumers would like to buy milk from cows that are not injected with bovine growth hormone. Doesn't it make sense to try to make our system respond to this market, to offer both kinds of milk and clearly label them so the buyer has a choice? Consumers with reasonable requests that don't currently fit into the system are simply patted on the head by scientists and policy makers, assured that all tests to date are negative and told not to worry.

Everyone agrees we want a safe food system but do we care about how the food is grown or its nutrition? If 60% of diseases are the result of poor diet, shouldn't agricultural and health policies be discussed together, somewhere and sometime?

Why are the words "efficiency" and "competitiveness" employed at every turn? Why not use inclusive accounting, so that long-term environmental, social and health issues are included in our national agricultural bookkeeping.

As farming becomes more efficient, so that fewer and fewer farmers are producing more food, will mixed-crop family farms survive? We know that one large vertically integrated poultry farm in Georgia could produce all the chicken eaten in Canada, but is this the future we want? What are the implications of such a scenario for our growers of cash crops, our feed dealers and our equipment sellers? Do we want to have locally grown food in Canada? Do we want to have farms in Canada?

We have more questions than answers. But we must struggle to understand what's happening and to make our food dollars speak for us at the checkout counter. We must work to strengthen rural and urban ties and create a better food system. Because, farmers and city folk alike, we are all consumers of food. Or, as Wendell Berry, the farmer philosopher, so eloquently said, "Eating is an agricultural act."

M.L.M.

BREADS AND GRAINS

EATING THE 5 TO 10 SERVINGS of grain recommended by Canada's Food Guide takes ingenuity. Rice, cereals, dumplings, pasta and noodles as well as bread need to be in our diet. Cereals such as rolled oats, millet, barley and wheat were traditionally served hot at breakfast — often with a sprinkling of flaxseed — but it's a rare household today that takes the time to cook them. Cold processed cereals have largely taken over because of their convenience. Unfortunately, the farmer gets only about 14 cents for the corn in a box of cornflakes. The rest of the money — about $4.14 — goes to pay for processing, packaging, transportation, promotion and retailing.

The traditional way for Canadians to eat grain is in the form of breads. During the waves of immigration in the late 19th century, Germans and Scandinavians brought their love of rye and pumpernickel, Eastern Europeans brought Easter breads and bagels and the Scottish brought scones. Now more recent immigrants from the Middle East have brought pita, South and Central Americans have brought tortillas and Caribbeans have brought roti.

Making bread is time consuming but rewarding. The latest kitchen gadget is a bread-making machine, but its appeal is a mystery to me. It turns out the product and the smell but without the tactile pleasures of kneading and shaping the dough.

If you find yourself at home on a rainy day, remember that flour and water can be transformed like magic into bread. It's especially nice to have company around at the end to enjoy the finished product.

Rubes, a store in the St. Lawrence Market in Toronto that specializes in bulk grains, stocks 30 different kinds of rice: Japanese sticky rice, purple and red rice from Thailand, aged basmati rice from Pakistan, brown short-grain rice from California, arborio rice from northern Italy and wild rice harvested from Canadian lakes.

Rice is an excellent source of complex carbohydrates. Served with small amounts of meat, legumes, nuts or seeds, it forms a complete protein.

While many Canadians serve rice occasionally as a substitute for pasta or potatoes, others eat it every day. A friend from India told me that buying rice is like buying a little bit of home. In India basmati rice might be used only once a week but here she is able to afford to eat it everyday. Basmati rice is slender, long grained and aged for a year after harvesting. It gives off a perfumed smell as it cooks.

Other grains are couscous used in African cooking, quinoa (pronounced keen-wa) and amaranth from South America, and bulgur used in the Middle East. These grains can be steamed and served as part of the main course.

M.L.M.

PIZZA

Most mothers find that their children love pizza. It's the most often requested recipe in cooking classes for new immigrants. Moms learn to make this Canadian treat and adapt it with spices, herbs and toppings from their own food culture.

DOUGH

The crust can be thin and crisp or thick and chewy, depending on your family's preference. If you live in the city, pizza dough is available in most bakeries or at the supermarket deli. Baked crusts can be found in the bread section.

1 cup warm water *250 mL*
pinch sugar
1 Tbsp dry active yeast *15 mL*
3½ cups flour *875 mL*
½ tsp salt *2 mL*
2 Tbsp olive oil *25 mL*

Mix warm water and sugar in large bowl; sprinkle with yeast. Let stand for 5 minutes.

Stir 2 cups (500 mL) of the flour and salt into yeast mixture, using a wooden spoon; beat until smooth. Let stand for 10 minutes. Stir in more of the flour (mixture will gradually pull away from sides of bowl. The amount of flour you use will vary depending on the weather and the protein in the flour. The idea is to get a ball that won't stick to your hands.) Turn dough out onto lightly floured board and let rest for 2 minutes. Wash out bowl and oil lightly.

Knead dough on floured board for about 10 minutes, sprinkling with flour as needed.

Put ball of dough in bowl and turn over so that it is lightly coated with oil. Cover with tea towel and put in warm place (the top of the refrigerator is ideal). Let rise for 1 hour.

(At this point dough can be punched down and allowed to rise again if you need more time, or punched down, lightly floured and refrigerated in a plastic bag for up to 2 days. Before baking, bring dough to room temperature.)

Punch down dough and knead for 2 minutes. Cut dough in half and roll out with a floured rolling pin (a floured wine bottle is a good substitute) on lightly floured board. Oil 2 baking sheets or pizza pans and form dough to fit.

Makes two 12 inch (30 cm) crusts.

▼ ▼ ▼ ▼ ▼ ▼ ▼ ▼ ▼ ▼ ▼ ▼ ▼ ▼ ▼ ▼

KNEADING KNOW-HOW

Flatten ball of dough slightly. Fold dough in half toward you and then push it away with the heels of both hands. Turn it one-quarter turn, fold and repeat. The dough will become shiny and elastic after about 10 minutes of kneading.

▲ ▲ ▲ ▲ ▲ ▲ ▲ ▲ ▲ ▲ ▲ ▲ ▲ ▲ ▲ ▲

TOPPINGS

The secret to a good pizza is a hot oven. Preheat oven to 450°F (230°C).

For a traditional pizza, top with tomato sauce and grated mozzarella cheese. For a new-style pizza, leave off the cheese and tomatoes, and spread with pesto.

Then add any combination of:
- sliced green or black olives, slivers of sweet red or green peppers, sliced mushrooms, pepperoni or bacon
- green peppers, ham and pineapple
- crumbled goat cheese and fresh basil
- black olives, anchovies and steamed broccoli florets
- eggplant cubes, red pepper slices and browned onions
- fontina, Asiago and mozzarella cheese with fresh basil
- artichoke hearts, whole garlic and shrimp

Bake on special ungreased pizza pans with holes or on lightly oiled baking sheets in the lower third of the oven for 15 to 20 minutes or until the crust is golden.

SHUSWAP BANNOCK

*Last winter, I worked on a committee of the Ontario
Native Women's Association with Gail Devlin, who shared
this traditional recipe with me. Prepared with blueberries,
this round bread makes a hearty breakfast treat.*

3 cups flour *750 mL*
1 Tbsp baking powder *15 mL*
1½ tsp salt *7 mL*
1½ cups water *375 mL*
1 cup blueberries (optional) *250 mL*

Stir 1 Tbsp (15 mL) of the flour into berries; set aside.
Mix remaining flour, baking powder and salt together in
large bowl. Make a well in centre of flour mixture and add
water all at once, stirring quickly. Stir in blueberry-flour mixture. Pour immediately into buttered 9 inch (23 cm) pie plate
and flatten with back of spoon. Bake at 450°F (230°C) for 20
to 25 minutes until golden brown and crusty on the outside.
Serve warm.

Makes 8 wedges.

▼ ▼ ▼ ▼ ▼ ▼ ▼ ▼ ▼ ▼ ▼ ▼ ▼ ▼

PLAIN BANNOCK

My family likes plain Bannock with soup. Use the
above recipe, but reduce water to 1¼ cups and omit
berries. Instead of pouring the batter directly into
the pie plate, knead 12 to 15 times on a floured surface. This alters the texture. Bake as you would
Shuswap Bannock

▲ ▲ ▲ ▲ ▲ ▲ ▲ ▲ ▲ ▲ ▲ ▲ ▲ ▲ ▲

BROWN SCONES

The brown sugar and sour cream in this recipe combine to add a complex and delightfully different flavour to these scones. For breakfast, Brown Scones are scrumptious warm from the oven spread with a little honey, butter or jam. For lunch or supper, they're a perfect companion to robust soups and salads.

1½ cups flour *375 mL*
½ cup bran *125 mL*
2 tsp baking powder *10 mL*
4 Tbsp brown sugar *60 mL*
½ tsp salt *2 mL*
4 Tbsp butter *60 mL*
½ cup sour cream *125 mL*
1 Tbsp milk *15 mL*

Mix together flour, bran, 3 Tbsp (45 mL) of the brown sugar, baking powder and salt.

Cut in butter until mixture has consistency of small peas.

Stir in sour cream. Transfer to lightly floured surface and knead about 8 times.

Pat into 8 inch (20 cm) round and cut into 12 wedges.

Mix remaining 1 Tbsp (15 mL) of the brown sugar and milk, and brush lightly over scones.

Bake at 425°F (220°C) for 12 minutes until golden.

Makes 12 scones

THE HARD FACTS ON FLOUR

Since medieval times, when white bread was a symbol of wealth and brown bread was the food of the poor, most flour has been bleached. However, we recommend using the unbleached variety, since bleaching is simply an unnecessary process done for aesthetic reasons. Unbleached flour has a pleasant off-white colour and is available in any natural food or bulk store. Hard flour, made from hard spring wheat, is ideal for making bread because its high percentage of gluten helps the dough to rise. Hard spring wheat, which grows on the Prairies and is able to withstand extreme temperatures, is planted in spring and harvested in late summer. Soft flour, on the other hand, is used in cakes and pastries where it gives a light delicate texture to the finished product. It's milled from soft winter wheat, which is planted in the fall (mostly in Ontario), spends the winter dormant and matures in summer. All-purpose flour, commonly sold in supermarkets, and used just as the name suggests, is a mixture of 75 percent hard and 25 percent soft flour. White flour has been sifted to remove the bran and germ but, in North America, vitamins must be added back, which is why it's called enriched. Whole wheat flour, on the other hand, includes all parts of the kernel (the endosperm, germ and bran). It contains vitamins A, B and E, protein and fat, but it needs to be stored in the refrigerator to prevent the germ from turning rancid. Baking with it requires some adjustment (use a little less whole wheat flour than the amount called for) since it gives a more dense result. For baked goods that are healthy without being heavy, try half white and half whole wheat flour.

▲ ▲ ▲ ▲ ▲ ▲ ▲ ▲ ▲ ▲ ▲ ▲ ▲ ▲ ▲ ▲ ▲

CURRANT SCONES

Quick and easy to prepare, this breakfast treat is sure to become a favourite of family and guests. Wild plum trees grow at the edge of our garden, and in alternate years when the crop is abundant, my husband and I make tart plum jelly — a heavenly topping for these scones. We also have a local apiary that supplies honey, which is wonderful drizzled over them.

4 cups flour *1 L*
2 Tbsp baking powder *25 mL*
2 Tbsp sugar *25 mL*
¾ tsp salt *4 mL*
1 cup cold butter *250 mL*
¾ cup currants *175 mL*
2 large eggs, lightly beaten
1 cup milk *250 mL*

Stir together flour, baking powder, sugar and salt in large bowl and mix well.

Cut in butter until mixture has consistency of small peas. Stir in currants.

With a fork, beat eggs and milk in small bowl. Pour over flour mixture, stirring with fork until soft, moist dough forms.

Turn dough onto lightly floured surface and knead gently about 15 to 20 times. Shape dough into ball. With sharp knife, cut in half.

On a baking sheet, pat each half into 8 inch (20 cm) circle, about ½ inch (1 cm) thick. Cut into 8 wedges as you would a pie (or 12, for smaller crispier servings).

Bake at 425°F (220°C) for 18 minutes or until golden brown. Serve warm.

Makes two 8 inch (20 cm) rounds.

No-Fuss Biscuits

Quick and easy, these drop biscuits make a wonderful accompaniment to soups and salads.

3 cups flour *750 mL*
2 Tbsp baking powder *25 mL*
½ tsp salt *2 mL*
¼ cup cold butter *50 mL*
1½ cups milk *375 mL*
¼ cup shredded Cheddar cheese (optional) *50 mL*

Sift together flour, baking powder and salt in bowl.

Cut in butter until mixture is consistency of small peas.

Stir in milk until dry ingredients are moistened; stir in Cheddar cheese (if using).

Drop from large soup spoon onto ungreased baking sheet.

Bake at 450°F (230°C) until golden and crisp on edges, about 18 minutes.

Makes 18 biscuits.

SPOON ROLLS

Spoon Rolls *require little time to prepare, other than the rising periods. Choose a day when you have other inside chores to do, and you'll be rewarded with a special treat at suppertime.* Spoon Rolls *are comfort food because of the wonderful yeasty smell that drifts from the kitchen as they're being made.*

1 package active dry yeast (or 1 Tbsp/15 mL)
¾ cup milk *175 mL*
⅓ cup shortening *75 mL*
¼ cup sugar *50 mL*
1 tsp salt *5 mL*
¼ cup cold water *50 mL*
1 egg, beaten
*4 cup*s flour *1 L*

Set yeast according to package directions.

Heat milk gently until skin forms on top.

Meanwhile, cream shortening, sugar and salt in large bowl. Stir scalded milk and cold water into shortening mixture, mixing well. Stir in beaten egg and yeast mixture. Stir in flour and knead, using additional flour, if needed, until smooth and shiny.

Cover bowl with tea towel and let rise in warm place about 2 hours.

Stir down and spoon into 2 buttered 9 inch (1.5 L) round

cake pans. Spoon dough into a ring around outside, and then into centre, being careful not to crowd because dough will expand as it rises.

Cover and let rise until volume has doubled, about 1 hour. Bake at 400°F (200°C) for 12 minutes until brown (rolls should sound hollow when flicked with your finger).

For soft rolls, brush with butter while still hot; for crustier rolls, serve just as they come from the oven.

Makes 30 rolls.

▼ ▼ ▼ ▼ ▼ ▼ ▼ ▼ ▼ ▼ ▼ ▼ ▼ ▼ ▼

Fresh Facts on Yeast

Yeast loses its potency and will not rise when it becomes stale. Yeast that's still active should foam and bubble when you add water to it. Keep only a small amount of yeast on hand, stored in a jar in the refrigerator.

▲ ▲ ▲ ▲ ▲ ▲ ▲ ▲ ▲ ▲ ▲ ▲ ▲ ▲ ▲ ▲

BERNICE'S SOURDOUGH
BISCUITS

*My mother-in-law, Bernice MacDonald, shared these
sourdough recipes years ago, and they immediately
became a staple at our house. Bernice's Sourdough
Biscuits, which are very fast because they need no rising
time, are good with any meal. Try them plain with butter, or for brunch, add jelly. For lunch, knead chopped
chives from the garden into the dough and serve with
soup. To serve with salad, knead in a little
shredded Cheddar cheese.*

½ *cup* flour *125 mL*
½ *cup* whole wheat flour *125 mL*
2 *tsp* baking powder *10 mL*
¼ *tsp* baking soda *1 mL*
¼ *tsp* salt *1 mL*
¼ *cup* butter *50 mL*
1 *cup* Sourdough Starter *250 mL*

Stir flours, baking powder, soda and salt together in bowl.
Cut in butter until mixture is consistency of peas. Stir in
Sourdough Starter.
Turn onto floured surface and knead until soft dough
forms. Pat out until about ½ inch (1 cm) thick and cut into

12 circles using cookie cutter or glass dipped in flour.

Bake on ungreased baking sheet at 425°F (220°C) for 12 minutes or until golden brown

Makes 12 biscuits.

▼ ▼ ▼ ▼ ▼ ▼ ▼ ▼ ▼ ▼ ▼ ▼ ▼ ▼

SOURDOUGH STARTER

To make: Dissolve 1 package of active dry yeast in ½ cup warm water. Stir in 2 cups of lukewarm water, 2 cups sifted flour, 1 teaspoon salt and 1 tablespoon sugar. Beat until smooth. Let stand, uncovered, at room temperature for 3 to 5 days, stirring 2 or 3 times daily, and covering at night. (Starter should have a yeasty, not sour, smell.) Cover and refrigerate until you're ready to use it.

Feeding the starter: After using part of the starter, you must replenish it. Mix 1 cup flour, 1 cup milk and ¼ cup sugar. Stir into the remaining Sourdough Starter and return it to the refrigerator. Even if you haven't used the starter, it should be fed every 10 days, using a half-batch of this recipe. I've kept the Sourdough Starter active in the refrigerator for months.

▲ ▲ ▲ ▲ ▲ ▲ ▲ ▲ ▲ ▲ ▲ ▲ ▲ ▲

BERNICE'S SOURDOUGH CORN BREAD

3 eggs
2½ cups buttermilk or sour milk *625 mL*
½ cup Sourdough Starter *125 mL*
½ cup cornmeal *125 mL*
2 Tbsp sugar *25 mL*
⅓ cup melted butter *75 mL*
¾ cup flour *175 mL*
2½ tsp baking powder *13 mL*
¾ tsp baking soda *4 mL*
1½ tsp salt *7 mL*

Whisk eggs in large bowl.

Stir in milk, *Sourdough Starter*, cornmeal and sugar. Stir in melted butter. Sift dry ingredients together and stir in.

Pour into buttered 13" x 9" (3.5 L) cake pan.

Bake at 450°F (230°C) for 30 to 35 minutes. Serve hot.

Makes 1 loaf.

PITA BREAD

*Pita is easy to buy but lots of fun to make. They puff up
like pillows, collapse and end up with a pocket inside.*

1 Tbsp dry active yeast *15 mL*
½ cup warm water *125 mL*
3½ cups flour *875 mL*
1 tsp salt *5 mL*
1 Tbsp olive oil *15 mL*
1 cup water *250 mL*

Dissolve yeast in warm water in large bowl. Stir in flour,
salt, oil and just enough of the water to make a firm dough.

Let rest for 5 minutes and then knead for about 10 minutes until dough is smooth and elastic. (See Kneading Know-
How on page 194.)

Place dough in clean bowl, cover and let rise in warm
place for about 2 hours. Punch down dough and let rise again
for about 1 hour.

Turn dough onto floured surface and roll it into a rope
about 2 inches (5 cm) in diameter. Cut in half, then cut each
half into 6 equal pieces.

Form each piece into a ball and roll each ball into a flattened 6 inch (15 cm) round. Let the 12 rounds rest on
floured surface while you proceed.

Preheat oven to 500°F (260°C) and set racks just below
middle of oven. Put heavy baking sheet into oven to heat up.

When oven is ready, using floured lifter, slide 3 rounds of dough onto hot baking sheet. Close oven door and if you have a glass window, watch the pitas puff up. They will cook in about 2 minutes.

Remove from oven and set on rack to collapse and cool. Repeat with remaining rounds.

Makes 12 pitas.

CHAPATI

*This unleavened Indian bread is delicious served hot with
vegetable or meat curries or dahl.*

2 cups whole wheat flour *500 mL*
½ cup warm water *125 mL*
2 tsp soft butter *10 mL*

Mix flour and water together in bowl to make stiff dough.
Stir in soft butter and knead dough on lightly floured surface
for about 10 minutes. (See Kneading Know-How on page
194.)

Roll dough into ball, cover with damp cloth and let rest
for 1 hour (dough can also be wrapped and refrigerated
overnight).

Knead dough at room temperature for 3 to 5 minutes.
Break off pieces the size of a golf ball. Flatten each ball with
your hands; using a rolling pin, roll each on lightly floured
surface into 8 inch (20 cm) rounds.

Heat ungreased cast-iron skillet until very hot. Cook one
chapati at a time. Put chapati on skillet for about 1 minute
until brown spots appear on underside; turn over and cook
on the other side for 1 minute. The chapati will puff up and
be lightly browned. Wrap chapatis in a clean tea towel to
keep warm.

Makes 8 chapatis.

▼

MEXICAN TORTILLAS

Masa harina, a corn meal treated with lime, is necessary to make tortillas. It can be found in most supermarkets. Although skill is needed to make perfectly round tortillas, this recipe is designed for the novice. With practice the dough can be shaped between the hands rather than with a rolling pin. Serve with refried beans, light sour cream, avocado and salsa.

2 cups masa harina *500 mL*
1⅛ cups water *280 mL*
salt
(vegetable oil)

Stir masa harina, water and salt together in bowl, first with fork and then with your hands.

Knead for 4 minutes until dough holds together. (See Kneading Know-How on page 194.)

Divide dough into 16 equal balls. Place a ball between two pieces of waxed paper and roll with rolling pin into 5 inch (15 cm) circles.

Heat ungreased cast iron skillet (or lightly oiled frying pan) and cook the tortilla for 45 seconds on each side. Flip back to first side and cook for another 45 seconds. Wrap in clean tea towel to keep warm.

Makes 16 tortillas.

TABBOULEH SALAD

Lots of parsley and mint give this Middle Eastern salad a summery taste. Great for lunches at work tabbouleh keeps well and can be made ahead. It's great. Bulgur is cracked wheat that has been steamed and dried.

¾ cup medium bulgur *175 mL*
1 cup boiling water *250 mL*
½ cup olive oil *125 mL*
¼ cup lemon juice *50 mL*
½ cup finely diced cucumber *125 mL*
½ red onion, minced
2 tomatoes, seeded and finely diced
salt and pepper
2 cups finely minced parsley *500 mL*
¼ cup finely minced mint *50 mL*

Pour boiling water over bulgur in bowl, cover with plate and let stand for about 30 minutes until water is absorbed.

Fluff with fork and drain off any excess water.

Stir olive oil and lemon juice into bulgur. Toss with fork.

Stir in cucumber, onion and tomatoes. Salt and pepper to taste. Stir in parsley and mint.

Makes 8 servings.

COUSCOUS WITH VEGETABLES

Lynda Murdoch contributed this recipe, given to her by one of the English as a Second Language students at the community college where she teaches. The real test of a successful recipe is its acceptance by kids and this one gets top marks from Lynda's family.

2 Tbsp oil 25 mL
½ cup chopped onion 125 mL
2 cloves garlic, minced
1 Tbsp grated fresh gingerroot 15 mL
1½ cups chicken stock 375 mL
2 cups peeled and cubed butternut or other hard squash 500 mL
½ tsp ground coriander 2 mL
½ tsp crushed chilies 2 mL
salt and pepper
1 zucchini
2 chopped tomatoes
1 can (19 oz/540 mL) chick peas
¼ cup chopped parsley 50 mL
1 cup couscous 250 mL
1 cup boiling water 250 mL

Heat oil in large skillet. Cook onion, garlic and ginger root until soft. Stir in stock and bring to a boil.

Add squash, coriander, chilies, salt and pepper; cook 5 to 7 minutes.

Cut zucchini into bite-sized pieces. Stir in zucchini, tomatoes, drained chick peas and parsley. Cook 2 to 3 minutes more.

Meanwhile boil water and pour over couscous. Cover for 5 minutes. Fluff with fork.

Pour vegetables and sauce over couscous and serve.

Makes 4 servings.

JOHNNY CAKE

The origins of the name are obscure. Some believe it's a distortion of the name of one of the First Nations who lived in the midwestern United States. Others believe that it comes from journey cake, because the flat bread was easy to carry when travelling. Some call thin corn-cakes "ponecakes," from the Algonquin word for corn, which is pone. For Johnny Cake *to be* Johnny Cake, *the recipe must include cornmeal; otherwise, there is consider-able variation. Sometimes they are quite plain, and are good served, like a bread, beside soups and salads; some-times they are a little richer and make a tasty dessert to end a homey meal. Great-aunt Julia, who lived across the garden path of my childhood farm, often served* Johnny Cake *and applesauce together.*

¾ cup light brown sugar *175 mL*
2 eggs, well beaten
2 cups sour cream *500 mL*
1½ cups flour *375 mL*
1 tsp baking soda *5 mL*
1½ cups cornmeal (preferably stone ground) *375 mL*

Cream sugar and eggs in bowl. Beat in sour cream, flour, cornmeal baking soda. Bake in greased 13" x 9" (3.5 L) bak-ing pan at 375°F (190°C) for 35 minutes or until cake pulls away from pan.

▼ ▼ ▼ ▼ ▼ ▼ ▼ ▼ ▼ ▼ ▼ ▼ ▼ ▼ ▼ ▼

GROUND CORN

Select stone-ground rather than machine-
ground corn, because the former process
retains the germ, along with its nutrients, and
the texture is nicer. Notice that, unlike flour,
cornmeal does not contain gluten, and therefore, cornbread does not rise or have the
same texture as breads made with
other grains.

▲ ▲ ▲ ▲ ▲ ▲ ▲ ▲ ▲ ▲ ▲ ▲ ▲ ▲ ▲ ▲

▼ ▼ ▼ ▼ ▼ ▼ ▼ ▼ ▼ ▼ ▼ ▼ ▼ ▼ ▼ ▼

QUICK BREADS

Quick breads are quick because they don't use
yeast as the leavening agent and so they don't
require rising time. They use either baking
powder or baking soda for the rising action.
With the exception of nut breads — which
benefit from storing overnight so that
flavours mellow — quick breads are generally
best served the same day they're baked.

▲ ▲ ▲ ▲ ▲ ▲ ▲ ▲ ▲ ▲ ▲ ▲ ▲ ▲ ▲ ▲

LEMON BREAD

*Lemon Bread has been a long-time family favourite.
My great-aunt liked to add half a cup of chopped walnuts
to the batter. I like Lemon Bread with poppy seeds,
accompanied by a fruity herbal tea. Little children like it
without poppy seeds or walnuts and spread with jelly.
Made plain, try serving it with mixed salad greens,
chunks of fresh fruit and a honey dressing.*

⅓ cup shortening or butter *75 mL*
1 cup sugar *250 mL*
2 eggs
1 Tbsp lemon juice (and grated peel, if you like) *15 mL*
1½ cups flour *375 mL*
1 tsp baking powder *5 mL*
¼ tsp salt *1 mL*
½ cup milk *125 mL*
½ cup chopped walnuts or poppy seeds (optional) *125 mL*

Cream shortening and sugar in bowl; beat in eggs. Stir in lemon juice and peel (if using).

Sift flour, baking powder and salt, and add alternately with milk to creamed mixture, beginning and ending with dry ingredients. Stir in walnuts or poppy seeds (if using). Pour into 9" x 5" (2 L) loaf pan.

Bake at 350°F (180°C) about 1 hour, until top is golden.

Makes 1 loaf.

FRESH CRANBERRY BREAD

*Cranberries arrive in markets and greengrocers in late
fall each year, most being transported from the more
moderate western seaboard areas. These slightly tart
berries are appreciated by those who dislike the usual rich
midwinter fare. While* Fresh Cranberry Bread *makes a
delicious addition to a company platter of dessert breads, it
is also very nice for a late breakfast, served with a mild
cheese. It is simple to make, looks wonderful
and tastes delicious.*

2 cups finely chopped fresh cranberries *500 mL*
2½ cups sugar
2 eggs, beaten lightly
⅓ cup butter *75 mL*
2 cups milk *500 mL*
5 cups flour *1.25 ml.*
2 tsp baking powder *10 ml.*
1 tsp salt *5 mL*
1 cup chopped walnuts (optional) *250 mL*

Mix cranberries with ½ cup (125 mL) of the sugar and set
aside.

Cream remaining sugar, eggs and butter in bowl. Stir in
milk.

Sift flour, baking powder and salt. Stir dry ingredients
into creamed mixture.

Stir in cranberries and walnuts (if using).

Turn into two greased 9" x 5" (2 L) loaf pans. Bake at 350°F (180°C) for 1 hour or until golden brown.

Makes 2 loaves.

▼ ▼ ▼ ▼ ▼ ▼ ▼ ▼ ▼ ▼ ▼ ▼ ▼ ▼ ▼

CRANBERRIES

Native to North America, cranberries are very high in vitamin C. To prevent scurvy, they were carried on ships in barrels of water and exported to Europe. They retain their nutritive value well, even when dried or frozen. You can make a quick cranberry relish by grinding cranberries, and mixing them with chopped apples and oranges, raisins and other dried fruits. Sweeten to taste with a little honey

▲ ▲ ▲ ▲ ▲ ▲ ▲ ▲ ▲ ▲ ▲ ▲ ▲ ▲ ▲

KITCHEN TABLE GRANOLA

Serve granola with fruit and milk for breakfast, or stir it into plain yogurt for a bedtime snack. In the kitchen, try substituting some granola for rolled oats in muffin and cookie recipes. For variety, try combining 6 cups (1.5) quick-cooking rolled oats with 4 cups (1 L) of the crunchier longer-cooking type.

1¼ cups vegetable oil *300 mL*
1¼ cups honey *300 mL*
10 cups rolled oats *2.5 L*
1 cup wheat germ *250 mL*
1 cup bran *250 mL*
1 cup sesame seeds *250 mL*
1 cup sunflower seeds *250 mL*
1 cup coconut *250 mL*
1 cup chopped nuts *250 mL*
¼ cup brewer's yeast *50 mL*
1 cup raisins *250 mL*

Heat oil and honey in small saucepan over medium heat. Stir into rolled oats, wheat germ, bran, sesame seeds, sunflower seeds, coconut, nuts and brewer's yeast in large roasting pan. Bake at 250°F (180°C) for 1 hour, stirring every 20 minutes. Cool. Stir in raisins. Store in glass jars or pottery containers.

▼ ▼ ▼ ▼ ▼ ▼ ▼ ▼ ▼ ▼ ▼ ▼ ▼ ▼ ▼ ▼

Apple and Granola Bake

Peel, pare and slice four large apples into a
shallow baking dish, and add half a cup of
orange juice; sprinkle about a cup of granola
over the top. Bake at 375°F (190°C) for 20 to
30 minutes, until the apples are tender.

▲ ▲ ▲ ▲ ▲ ▲ ▲ ▲ ▲ ▲ ▲ ▲ ▲ ▲ ▲ ▲

▼ ▼ ▼ ▼ ▼ ▼ ▼ ▼ ▼ ▼ ▼ ▼ ▼ ▼ ▼ ▼

Nuts & Seeds

Because nuts and seeds can become rancid,
you should store them in tightly capped jars
in the refrigerator. Their flavours are cap-
tured in their essential oils. When they're
over-dry and withered, nuts and seeds have
lost much of their flavour. These foods are
high in both protein and fats.

▲ ▲ ▲ ▲ ▲ ▲ ▲ ▲ ▲ ▲ ▲ ▲ ▲ ▲ ▲ ▲

RISOTTO

Using a unique cooking method, short-grained arborio rice from northern Italy is sautéed in olive oil and butter. Hot broth is added a little at a time. The pot is stirred almost constantly as the liquid reduces and more broth is added and absorbed until the rice is cooked. At the last minute, asparagus tips and Parmesan cheese are added. Since risotto must be prepared at the last minute and takes about 25 minutes, it can become part of the dinner entertainment.

2 *cups* arborio rice *500 g*
6 *cups* chicken or vegetable broth *1.5 L*
2 *Tbsp* butter *25 mL*
4 *Tbsp* olive oil *60 mL*
1 small onion, minced
1 clove garlic, minced
½ *cup* dry white wine *125 mL*
1 *tsp* saffron threads *5 mL*
½ *lb* asparagus *250 g*
1 *cup* grated Parmesan cheese
salt and pepper to taste

Wash and drain rice.

Heat broth and keep at a simmer so that it will be hot when added to the rice.

Heat oil and 1 Tbsp (15 mL) butter and olive oil until

foaming in pot over medium-high heat. Reduce heat to medium and add onion and garlic. Cook until softened but not brown. Add rice and stir until all grains are coated. Stir in white wine and cook, stirring, until wine has been absorbed into rice.

Add ½ cup (125 mL) of hot broth, stirring until liquid is absorbed. Dissolve saffron threads in next ½ cup (125 mL) broth. Continue adding broth, ½ cup (125 mL) at a time, stirring almost constantly. You may need more or less liquid than recipe calls for. Use hot water if more liquid is necessary. Cook rice until creamy but not wet. Rice is ready when it is tender, firm and sticky but not soupy

Meanwhile cut asparagus into 1 inch (2.5 cm) pieces and steam until just tender, about 4 minutes.

Add asparagus, cheese, remaining 1 Tbsp (15 mL) butter and salt and pepper to the rice. Serve immediately.

Makes 6 to 8 side-dish servings or 4 to 6 main-dish servings .

▼ ▼ ▼ ▼ ▼ ▼ ▼ ▼ ▼ ▼ ▼ ▼ ▼ ▼ ▼

THE LONG AND SHORT OF RICE

Rice is easy to digest, cholesterol-free, gluten-free, low in sodium, non-allergenic and contains only a trace of fat. Each kernel has an outer layer of bran and inner layer of germ. Rice is a good source of fibre, calcium, B vitamins, iron and phosphorous. Short-grain rice is very absorbent and soft when cooked. It tends to stick together and is the preferred rice for puddings and dishes with sauces. Long-grain rice, whose kernels are firm and separate, is ideal for serving on its own.

COOKING METHOD

Rinse 1 cup (250 mL) of rice in bowl of cold
water until the water is clear. Drain well.
For brown rice, bring 2 cups (500 mL) of
salted water to boil. Add rice and bring back
to boil. Cover and simmer for 45 minutes (do
not remove cover while cooking). Yields 3 to
4 cups (750 mL to 1 L) of cooked rice.
For white rice, bring 1½ cups (375 mL) of
salted water to boil. Add rice and bring back
to boil. Cover and simmer for 20 minutes (do
not remove cover while cooking). Yields 3
cups (750 mL) of cooked rice.

TYPES OF RICE

Basmati rice, from India, Pakistan and Iran, is
a slender long-grain rice that is aged for a year
after harvesting. This aging develops the aro-
matic scent that it gives off during cooking.
Italian aborio rice, from the Po Valley in
Northern Italy, is a short-grain starchy rice
used in risottto. It's creamy yet firm.
White rice, which has the bran and germ
removed from the kernel, is the most popular
rice and stores well. Parboiled or converted
rice retains many of the nutrients of brown
rice during its processing. Brown rice is nutty,
chewy and nutritionally superior to white
rice. Since it has enzymes that can cause it to
turn rancid, it should be stored in the
refrigerator from 3 to 6 months.

▲ ▲ ▲ ▲ ▲ ▲ ▲ ▲ ▲ ▲ ▲ ▲ ▲ ▲

RICE PUDDING

When serving rice as a vegetable for dinner, cook extra and set aside 2 cups (500 mL) in order to make Rice Pudding. *While there are quicker ways to make rice pudding, this will become a favourite — for dessert, a bed-time snack, or made especially for a late brunch and served with cinnamon toast.*

4 cups milk *1 L*
4 eggs, beaten
2 cups cooked rice *500 mL*
1 cup sugar *250 mL*
½ cup raisins *125 mL*
1 tsp nutmeg *5 mL*

Whisk milk and eggs in bowl.
Stir in rice, sugar, raisins and nutmeg.
Pour into 8 cup (2 L) baking dish and bake at 325°F (160°C) for 1 hour or until custard has set.

Makes 8 servings.

HARVEST &
CELEBRATION
SWEETS

CELEBRATING THE HARVEST

FOR MILLENNIA, people around the world have celebrated the harvest. It guarantees, after all, survival. With each season, culminating with the autumn, we celebrate the productivity of the earth and the fruits of our labour.

Each summer, thousands of workers bring in the Canadian harvest, many from offshore. Most arrive when the harvest begins in late spring and leave when frost comes calling in the autumn, but some work up to eight months. In 1993, over 11,000 men and women laboured in Canada under bilateral agreements that Canada enjoys with Mexico and Commonwealth Caribbean countries, Of these, over 10,000 worked in Ontario's fields and orchards, addressing an historical seasonal shortage of workers during the short, intense season when the crops ripen.

Ontario boasts two particularly productive areas for growing tender fruits, each enjoying eco-systems moderated by the Great Lakes. In summer, the branches of fruit trees are weighed down with juicy peaches and ripening vineyards exude the aroma of summer. Essex County, one of these areas, extends southward, reaching the same latitude as Rome, the Mediterranean and northern California. This peninsula of land, bounded on three sides by Lake Erie, the Detroit River and Lake St. Clair, enjoys one of the most temperate climates in Canada. The other area the Niagara Peninsula, which is bounded on three sides by Lake Erie, the

Niagara River and Lake Ontario, also boasts similar harvests. The waters moderate temperatures, and along the shoreline, orchards grow and fruits ripen in lush abundance in the humid, muggy atmosphere.

Less tolerant eco-systems that won't sustain tender fruits will often support cherry, apple and pear trees and strawberry farms. Harsher climates bear winter-hardy rhubarb, currants, blueberries and some varieties of raspberries. Our farm in eastern Ontario produces wild strawberries, bramble berries and gooseberries — although the birds often enjoy the fruits before we get to them with our baskets.

Once the crops were harvested by farm families, supplemented with labour from nearby towns and villages. But as well-paid manufacturing jobs and the low unemployment rate in Ontario made local seasonal labour difficult to come by, farmers brought in Quebecers and Maritimers to pick and package the harvest for market. In more recent years, it has been Mexican and Jamaican labourers who have arrived to climb orchard ladders, stoop over berries, ride the harvesting machines and sort and package in the barns.

Although employers must register their needs weeks in advance of the harvest with local government employment offices who conduct a search locally before approval is granted to import workers, off-shore labour remains a controversial issue. Bringing in the harvest is hard work, and some maintain that local people no longer want to sweat from dawn to dusk during the compressed harvesting season. Others simply observe that the number of permits goes up in years when domestic unemployment is low and down when people need work, a standard supply and demand situation.

Nevertheless, year after year, the same labourers return, some with their families, to spend three, four or five months, harvesting vegetables and labour-intensive tender fruits. The few who organize the harvest come earlier and stay later, preparing barns and lodgings and checking equipment and supplies. Afterward, they wrap up loose ends for another season. These few weeks of summertime work provide money that goes a long way toward ensuring livable annual income in the migrants' home countries.

K.M.

A Lesson in Baking

HELEN IRWIN, WHO LIVES in a village in southwestern Ontario and belongs to the Ontario Farm Women's Network, shares a delightful story, one that seems universal. Many of us learned to cook in this way, following the less-than-specific directions of grandmothers, mothers or aunts.

Helen writes: My grandmother, Helen Hedges, was born in Haldimand County in 1860 and lived to be over 100. She was a renowned cook, especially for her cookies: sugar, plain, cinnamon, raisin, currant, hickory or black walnut, date-filled and oatmeal — all made from one basic recipe. When she was in her late seventies I asked her for the recipe and this is how our conversation went:

"Oh, cookies are no bother at all. First, you put some bread flour in a big bowl.

By bread flour, she meant hard wheat flour, not pastry flour. Flour, then, was flour with no additives.

"How much flour?"

"That all depends on how many cookies you want to make. Add three-quarters to a cup of sugar."

"How do you know exactly how much sugar, and should it be brown or white?"

"Do you want to make brown sugar cookies or white sugar cookies? Put in enough for the flour you have. Then, an egg or two according to the size of the eggs and how many cookies you are making, but don't overdo eggs. Add a pinch or so of salt, and the baking powder. If the milk is sour, use soda."

"How much baking powder?"

"Oh, use your judgment — a spoonful or two [teaspoon, she meant]. If the flour is new, add another just to be on the safe side, but too much spoils the flavour. Never use new flour if you can get out of it. The fat should be soft, so rub it in with a stir, just enough to slightly mix it."

Today, flour does not have to age as it did then. She claimed newly milled flour wasn't fit to use before February. I asked what kind of fat she used.

"I like fresh pork drippings best, but that tends to go off flavour in the summertime. Or part beef fat is good unless you cooked it with onion. Chicken fat is good, too, but that burns easily, so watch your oven. Chicken fat is very rich so reduce the amount about a quarter. Never use butter — it's too rich and heavy." She was elderly before she ever bought lard or shortening — and she claimed it was no good at all.

I asked how much fat she used.

"Oh, just put in enough to make a rich dough, about half as much as for pie crust. But use stiffer fat for pie crust. Now add a bit of milk, enough to make a soft dough, but stiff enough that it doesn't stick to a well-floured bake board. Roll it out, not too thick, and there you are. You can add some nuts or raisins, if you like, or stick a big, fat seeded raisin in the centre of each. Or sprinkle the tops with sugar. Use lemon flavouring for a change."

I asked her about oatmeal cookies.

"Oatmeal? I like the big, thick flakes. Reduce the flour some, that's all."

Explicit instructions, indeed. But my mother claimed that was far more than she received when it was her turn to learn to make cookies. My mother's cookies were good enough, but never up to my grandmother's standards, concludes Helen.

Reading Helen's recollection of learning to bake cookies reminded me of my own attempts to duplicate my grandmother's fantastic date-filled sugar cookies. It seemed effortless for her to mix a perfect batter without measuring a single ingredient. She went by consistency. First, she would cream together eggs, sugar and butter. Then she would sift the flour, baking powder and sugar. She would add this dry mixture alternately with the milk. Going by instinct and practice, she might add a little more flour or a splash more of milk. In the same easy manner, she prepared the date filling in a saucepan on top of the stove, putting dates, boiling water and a pinch of baking soda together. Every time, the filling was perfect — neither too thick nor too thin for spreading.

While I could never repeat the success of my grandmother's cookies, I did develop a casual attitude in the kitchen. The recipes that follow are not delicate. Within reason, they survive substitutions and will still turn out delicious. If you don't use butter and prefer shortening, substitute it. If you prefer all-purpose flour to unbleached hard flour, substitute it. If you prefer pecans to walnuts, your dessert should still turn out fine.

My casual attitude in the kitchen extends to the dining table. Whether it's a homey get-together with close friends or a more festive celebration, I'm likely to serve simple desserts created from a generous harvest. Nearly all of the following recipes come from the old-fashioned farm cooking that I know so well. Desserts like *Peach Crumble Pie*, *Fresh Apple Cake* and *Grandma's Fruit Pudding* evoke comfort food and rural traditions with great gusto. Healthful and satisfying, these recipes celebrate the bounty of fruits that we're blessed with every year. I hope they become part of your family celebrations, too.

K.M.

FRUIT PLATTER WITH WONDERFUL WHIPPED DIP

*Karen Motruk, my daughter, likes this easy dip because it
takes so little time to prepare. The farming country
where Karen lives produces abundant harvests of melons
and strawberries. Both are especially good with this dip.
Fruit platters are ideal finger foods, so cut fruits into an
appropriate size and serve with a dish of toothpicks. To
prevent fruits — such as apples and pears — from turning dark when cut up, drench them for a few minutes in
a mixture of ¼ cup (50 mL) lemon juice and ¾ cup (175
mL) water before placing on the platter.*

2 cups	whipping cream	500 mL
8 oz	cream cheese, soft	500 g
1 cup	icing sugar	250 mL

½ lemon, squeezed

cinnamon

In chilled bowl, whip cream until soft peaks form.
In another bowl, beat cream cheese.
Beat in icing sugar and lemon juice.
Add whipping cream and beat together until smooth.
Sprinkle with pinch of cinnamon.

DIVINE FRUIT DIP

Divine Fruit Dip *is a bit of heaven on your palate when served with kiwifruit, grapes, bananas, pears and apples.*

Stir 2 tablespoons of brown sugar and half a teaspoon of vanilla into 2 cups of sour cream or plain yogurt. Sprinkle with a pinch of nutmeg if you like.

▼ ▼ ▼ ▼ ▼ ▼ ▼ ▼ ▼ ▼ ▼ ▼ ▼ ▼ ▼

YOGURT

Yogurt is a Turkish name and it's an important food in that culture. It is also common throughout the Middle East and India. When fermenting bacteria combines with warm milk (and is kept warm for several hours), the lactose is lowered, which means that even people who can't digest milk can usually enjoy yogurt. Most cultures around the world have developed a process for thickening milk — sometimes sheep, goat or donkey, as well as the more common cow's milk. People who make their own yogurt often save some (like those who keep a sourdough starter), which they add to the next batch in order to start it working. Most yogurts are lower in fat than sour cream, and yogurt provides a fresh, slightly tart flavour that's less heavy and rich than sour cream. Yogurt can be substituted for sour cream, sour milk or buttermilk in most recipes.

▲ ▲ ▲ ▲ ▲ ▲ ▲ ▲ ▲ ▲ ▲ ▲ ▲ ▲ ▲

FRUIT COMPOTES

Fruit compotes make a deliciously light ending to a meal. Select three or four ripe fruits whose colours and textures complement one another. There are no rules for making this — you use what you have on hand — although in berry season, strawberries, raspberries and blackberries, drizzled with lime juice, make a delicious combination. For variation, you can substitute the fruit and juice of a grapefruit or the juice of two limes for the lemon juice.

¼ cup lemon juice *50 mL*
4 cups chopped seasonal fruits *1 L*
½ cup apple or orange juice *125 mL*
maple syrup (optional)

Pour lemon juice into glass serving bowl.

Halve fruits like cherries and grapes and remove pits. Remove peel from peaches, but leave it on pears and apples, which need only to be cored and chopped into bite-sized pieces. In season, include strawberries and raspberries. Melons are also a popular addition. Put chopped fruit into serving bowl.

Pour apple juice over fruit and stir gently so as not to bruise fruit. Let stand for about 30 minutes before serving to allow flavours to mellow.

Makes 4 to 6 servings.

RHUBARB & STRAWBERRY CRUMBLE

Most farms and many city backyards have a rhubarb patch. According to folklore, rhubarb has medicinal bene-fits as a spring tonic; the stalks were stewed with a little sugar to make them easier to swallow. Rhubarb is ready for picking about the time strawberries ripen in June, and often the two early fruits team up to make jam, pie or this delicious dessert.

¼ *cup* butter *125 mL*
1 *cup* flour *250 mL*
¾ *cup* quick-cooking rolled oats *175 mL*
¾ *cup* light brown sugar *175 mL*
1 *tsp* cinnamon *5 mL*
¼ *tsp* nutmeg *2 mL*
¼ *tsp* salt *2 mL*
2 *cups* chopped rhubarb,
cut into ½ inch (1 cm) pieces *500 mL*
2 *cups* halved strawberries *500 mL*
⅔ *cup* white sugar *150 mL*
2 *Tbsp* cornstarch *25 mL*
2 *Tbsp* lemon juice *25 mL*
boiling water
1 *tsp* vanilla *5 mL*

Melt butter in saucepan over low heat. Let cool slightly.

Stir in flour, oats, brown sugar, cinnamon, nutmeg and salt until crumbly.

Press half of the mixture into buttered 9 inch (2.5 L) baking dish. Cover with chopped fruit.

Mix white sugar and cornstarch in saucepan. Add enough boiling water to lemon juice to make 1 cup (250 mL). Stir in lemon juice–boiling water mixture and cook, stirring, until thick, about 15 minutes.

Remove from heat and stir in vanilla.

Pour evenly over fruit. Sprinkle with remaining flour mixture and pat lightly with back of wooden spoon.

Bake at 325°F (160°C) for 50 to 60 minutes or until bubbly and golden.

Serve warm with a scoop of ice cream.

Makes 4 to 6 servings.

APPLE CRISP

Fruit crisps are easy to prepare and almost any fruit can
be substituted for the apples — cherries are especially
good. Served with ice cream, a hot crisp is
wonderfully satisfying.

½ cup brown sugar *125 mL*
⅓ cup flour *75 mL*
1 tsp cinnamon *5 mL*
¼ tsp nutmeg *1 mL*
salt
¼ cup cold butter *50 mL*
¼ cup orange juice *50 mL*
6 large apples, peeled, cored and sliced

Combine sugar, flour, cinnamon, nutmeg and salt in bowl.

Cut in butter with pastry cutter until mixture is the size of small peas.

Stir in juice with a fork.

Arrange apple slices in 9 inch (23 cm) pie plate, and sprinkle with topping.

Bake at 375°F (190°C) for 45 minutes, covering if topping begins to brown before apples are tender.

Makes 6 servings.

PEACH CRUMBLE PIE

In August, when peaches are plentiful and ripe, indulge in this divine dessert. For a nutty variation, stir ½ cup (125 mL) chopped pecans into the peach mixture. Use your favourite pastry recipe for the single-crust pie shell.

pastry for single-crust pie
5 cups peeled, thinly sliced peaches *1.25 L*
¾ cup white sugar *175 mL*
¾ cup flour *175 mL*
2 tsp cinnamon *10 mL*
pinch salt
¾ cup brown sugar *175 mL*
¾ cup rolled oats *175 mL*
½ cup butter *125 mL*

Roll out pastry on floured surface and fit into 9 inch (23 cm) pie plate.

Stir together peaches, white sugar, ¼ cup (50 mL) of the flour, ½ tsp (2 mL) of the cinnamon and salt in bowl; spoon into pie shell. Combine brown sugar, rolled oats, remaining ½ cup (125 mL) of the flour and remaining 1½ tsp (7 mL) of the cinnamon in bowl. Cut in butter with pastry cutter until mixture is size of peas. Sprinkle over peach mixture. Bake at 350°F (180°C) for 30 minutes until peaches are tender and topping is lightly browned.

Makes 6 servings.

COUNTRY FAVOURITE
BUTTER PASTRY

This rich pastry is delicious and perfect for desserts.

1½ *cups* flour *375 mL*
1 *Tbsp* sugar *15 mL*
dash salt
½ *cup* cold butter *125 mL*
½ *Tbsp* vinegar *7 mL*
4½ *Tbsp* ice water *70 mL*

Mix flour, sugar and salt in shallow bowl. With pastry cutter, cut in butter until mixture is consistency of small peas and corn meal. Mix together vinegar and ice water; sprinkle 2 Tbsp (25 mL) over flour-butter mixture, stirring with fork to moisten. (Depending on the type of flour you've used, the mixture may hold together. If not, add remaining liquid.)

Using your hands, form pastry into ball. On floured surface, using rolling pin, roll pastry into circle large enough to extend ½ inch (1 cm) beyond the edge of pie plate. Roll pastry over rolling pin and transfer to pie plate. To neatly finish the edges, fold edges under and flute pastry by forming it over your index finger in a series of ruffles around the edge of pie plate.

Makes enough for a single-crust pie.

RASPBERRY CHEESECAKE

For an attractive, delectable treat, I serve this cheesecake on a pedestal plate that my father bought at a country auction years ago. It's not only eye-pleasing, it's delicious.

CRUST
1 ¼ cups flour *300 mL*
¼ tsp salt *1 mL*
⅓ cup + 2 Tbsp cold butter *100 mL*
3 *Tbsp* orange liqueur (or cold water) *45 mL*

FILLING
1 *lb* cream cheese, softened *500 g*
½ cup light cream *125 mL*
½ cup sugar *125 mL*
3 eggs
1 tsp vanilla *5 mL*

TOPPING
1 cup sour cream *250 mL*
1 *Tbsp* sugar *15 mL*
2 cups fresh or frozen raspberries *500 mL*
¼ cup currant jelly, melted *50 mL*

CRUST: Stir flour and salt together in bowl; cut in butter using pastry cutter until mixture is consistency of peas. Stir in orange liqueur. Mixture should hold together; if necessary, add extra liquid, a little at a time, until desired consistency. Pat crust into buttered 10 inch (3 L) springform pan. Place in freezer for 30 minutes. While crust is chilling, prepare filling.

FILLING: Beat cream cheese and cream in bowl until very smooth. Beat in sugar. Beat in eggs and vanilla; stir well. Pour over chilled crust and bake at 350°F (180°C) for 40 to 45 minutes until filling is set. Remove from oven; immediately spread with topping.

TOPPING: Stir sour cream and sugar together in bowl. Spread over cheesecake and return to oven for an additional 5 minutes. Remove from oven. Top with raspberries and drizzle with melted jelly. Cool. Just before serving, remove sides of springform pan, and place cake on serving dish.

Makes 8 to 10 servings.

APPLESAUCE

Aunt Julia used to make applesauce with windfalls — the ripe apples that fall off the tree before the harvesting team can pick them from the branches. And she never peeled them. Instead, she had an applesauce sieve: a cone-shaped affair that came with a wooden instrument that looked a bit like a rolling pin with one end tapered to a point. After the apples were cooked, she pushed the sauce through the sieve with the tapered wooden tool. If you don't have an applesauce sieve, put the cooked apples through a food mill or sieve to remove the peel.

3 lb apples, cored and sliced (about 12) 1.5 kg
½ Tbsp lemon juice 7 mL
pinch salt
1 2-inch (5 cm) cinnamon stick (optional)
brown sugar (optional)

Put apples, lemon juice, salt and cinnamon stick (if using) in heavy saucepan, adding about ½ inch (1 cm) water to prevent sticking. Cover and cook over medium-low heat for about 20 minutes, stirring occasionally and adding more water if necessary to prevent sticking or drying out (fresh apples have more moisture than older ones).

Taste and add spoonful of brown sugar if desired (some apples are quite sweet and need no sugar).

Put through food mill or sieve. Wonderful served warm.

Makes 4 to 6 servings.

BAKED APPLES

*This may be the easiest dessert of all to make and it's a
favourite that never goes out of style.*

2 large baking apples, halved and cored
2 *Tbsp* brown sugar *25 mL*
2 *Tbsp* raisins *25 mL*
½ *tsp* cinnamon *2 mL*
dash nutmeg
pinch cloves
½ *cup* water *125 mL*

Arrange apples, core side up, in shallow baking dish or
small pie plate.

Mix sugar, raisins and spices in small bowl.

Pack sugar mixture into hollows from coring. Pour water
into dish.

Bake at 375°F (190°C) for 25 minutes or until soft. Serve
warm with the syrupy juices poured over baked apples.

Makes 2 to 4 servings.

▼ ▼ ▼ ▼ ▼ ▼ ▼ ▼ ▼ ▼ ▼ ▼ ▼ ▼

APPLE LORE

The apple harvest occurs from late summer
through late autumn. Many different varieties
are grown in Canada. Some are best eaten
raw; others are produced for cooking; still
other all-purpose varieties exhibit marvellous
versatility, being suitable for nibbling and
baking. Raw apples, which are said to aid
digestion, bring to mind the old adage, "An
apple a day keeps the doctor away." A medi-
um-size fresh apple contains about 70 calories
while a sweetened baked apple has about 190
calories. Most of the vitamins and minerals in
apples are concentrated directly under the
peel. Therefore, baking apples in their jackets
(or when making applesauce, cooking with
the peel on and pushing the pulp through a
sieve afterwards) ensures the maximum
nutritional benefit.

▲ ▲ ▲ ▲ ▲ ▲ ▲ ▲ ▲ ▲ ▲ ▲ ▲ ▲ ▲

APPLE PUDDING

*This old-fashioned treat is delicious sprinkled with icing
sugar and served with cream.*

2 eggs
½ *cup* milk *125 mL*
½ *cup* flour *125 mL*
¼ *tsp* salt *1 mL*
3 tart apples, peeled, cored, and sliced
4 *Tbsp* butter *60 mL*

Beat together eggs, milk, flour, and salt in bowl until smooth.

Stir in apple slices.

Melt butter in 8 inch (2 L) cake pan. Pour batter into pan.

Bake at 425°F (220°C) for 30 minutes or until the top is brown and crisp.

Spoon into serving dishes.

Makes 4 servings.

FRESH APPLE CAKE

*Serve this fine fall dessert warm with whipped cream, or
smothered in* Cream Cheese Icing, *for a hearty
finale to a meal.*

2 *cups* flour *500 mL*
2 *cups* sugar *500 mL*
2 *tsp* baking soda *10 mL*
1 *tsp* cinnamon *5 mL*
½ *tsp* nutmeg *2 mL*
½ *tsp* salt *2 mL*
4 *cups* peeled, cored, finely diced apples (about 1½ lb/750 g)
½ *cup* chopped walnuts *125 mL*
½ *cup* butter, soft *125 mL*
2 eggs

Sift dry ingredients together in bowl.

Stir in apples and nuts.

In another bowl, cream butter and eggs together; stir into
apple mixture until just combined (batter will be thick).

Bake at 350°F (180°C) in buttered 13" x 9" (3.5 L) cake
pan for 1 hour.

Makes 12 generous servings.

CREAM CHEESE ICING

4 oz soft cream cheese *125 g*
2 Tbsp butter *25 mL*
1 tsp vanilla *5 mL*
2 cups sifted icing sugar *500 mL*

Beat cream cheese and butter until smooth.
Stir in vanilla. Gradually beat in icing sugar.
If chocolate icing is desired, substitute 1/4 to 1/3 cup (50 to 75 mL) sifted unsweetened cocoa powder for some of the icing sugar.
If icing is too thick, add milk a tablespoon at a time to thin it; if icing is too thin, add a little more icing sugar.

Makes enough for a large cake.

APPLE MINCEMEAT PIE

*It's not as rich or heavy as mincemeat pie but it's a fruity
variation that leaves you with a satisfied stomach.*

pastry for double-crust pie
(see recipe on page 48)
2 cups sliced cored peeled apples *500 mL*
2 Tbsp flour *25 mL*
2 cups Green Tomato Mincemeat *500 mL*
(see recipe on page 177)

Roll out half of pastry and fit into 9 inch (23 cm) pie
plate.

Dust apple slices with flour; gently combine with mincemeat. Spoon into pie shell.

Roll out remaining pastry and fit on top of pie; slash
steam vents.

Bake at 400°F (200°C) for 40 to 45 minutes.

Makes 8 servings.

BLUEBERRY SPICE COFFEE CAKE

*Blueberries grow wild in eastern and northern Canada;
children sit at roadside stands in July, hawking the
berries that are found among the rocky outcroppings.
Some varieties are also grown commercially and available
at markets. Out of season, you can use frozen blueberries.*

1 cup blueberries (fresh or frozen) *250 mL*
2 Tbsp white sugar *25 mL*
2 Tbsp balsamic vinegar *25 mL*
1½ cups flour *375 mL*
½ cup brown sugar *125 mL*
1 tsp baking soda *5 mL*
1 tsp ground ginger *5 mL*
¼ tsp cinnamon *1 mL*
¼ tsp mace *1 mL*
½ cup sour cream *125 mL*
2 eggs, lightly beaten
½ cup vegetable oil *125 mL*
2 Tbsp corn syrup *25 mL*
icing sugar

Combine blueberries, white sugar and balsamic vinegar
in bowl. Stir gently and let stand for 1 hour. Strain, reserving
juices.

Mix together flour, brown sugar, baking soda and spices; set aside.

Combine reserved juices and sour cream in large bowl. Beat in eggs, oil and corn syrup.

Stir in flour mixture gradually until smooth. Pour two-thirds of the batter into buttered 9 inch (3 L) tube pan. Spread drained berries over batter.

Top with remaining batter — it won't completely cover and berries will poke through.

Bake at 350°F (180°C) for 35 to 40 minutes until the cake begins to pull away from sides of pan.

Remove cake from pan when slightly cooled. Sift with icing sugar. Serve warm.

Makes 8 servings.

PUMPKIN MUFFINS

*In the fall, when you carve the jack o' lantern for
Hallowe'en, make a pumpkin purée in the same way you
make applesauce (see recipe on page 243). When fresh
pumpkin isn't available, canned pumpkin purée works
fine in these delicious muffin treats.*

2 cups pastry flour *500 mL*
½ tsp salt *2 mL*
½ tsp baking soda *2 mL*
1 Tbsp baking powder *15 mL*
1 tsp cinnamon *5 mL*
¼ tsp mace *1 mL*
¼ tsp ground cloves *1 mL*
⅓ cup raisins *75 mL*
⅓ cup chopped almonds or walnuts (optional) *75 mL*
1 cup pumpkin purée *250 mL*
⅓ cup corn syrup *75 mL*
½ cup milk *125 mL*
2 eggs, beaten
½ cup vegetable oil *125 mL*

Sift dry ingredients into large bowl. Stir in raisins and
nuts; set aside.

Beat pumpkin purée, corn syrup, milk, eggs and oil in
bowl.

Make a well in centre of dry ingredients and pour in

pumpkin mixture. Stir just until dry ingredients are moistened.

Drop by spoonfuls into buttered muffin tins.

Bake at 400°F (200°C) for 20 minutes or until golden brown. Turn out. Serve warm.

Makes 18 muffins.

▼ ▼ ▼ ▼ ▼ ▼ ▼ ▼ ▼ ▼ ▼ ▼ ▼ ▼ ▼

MUFFINS

For perfect muffins, do not over-mix the batter. They should be shiny, golden brown and evenly rounded. If you overbeat, the muffins will be dull, probably peaked and tough.

▲ ▲ ▲ ▲ ▲ ▲ ▲ ▲ ▲ ▲ ▲ ▲ ▲ ▲ ▲

Warm Pumpkin
Cheesecake

Inspired by warm pumpkin cheesecake I enjoyed in a little vegetarian restaurant in Ann Arbor, Michigan, I created this recipe using pumpkin from our farm, but it works equally well with store-bought pure pumpkin purée.

Crust
1 ¼ cups graham wafer crumbs *300 mL*
⅓ cup butter, melted *75 mL*
1 Tbsp white sugar *15 mL*

Combine crumbs, melted butter and sugar. Press into buttered 9 inch (23 cm) springform pan. Put into freezer.

Filling
1 lb cream cheese *500 g*
¾ cup brown sugar *175 mL*
1 Tbsp lemon juice *15 mL*
4 large eggs
1 cup sour cream *250 mL*
1 cup pumpkin purée *250 mL*
1 tsp cinnamon *5 mL*
½ tsp nutmeg *2 mL*
¼ tsp ground cloves *1 mL*
pinch allspice

Beat cream cheese and sugar in bowl. Beat in lemon juice and eggs, one at a time.

Beat in sour cream, pumpkin and spices, mixing thoroughly. Pour into prepared crust and bake at 350°F (180°C) for 1 hour.

Turn oven off, but leave cheesecake inside for about 45 minutes, allowing it to cool with oven door ajar. (The cheesecake will finish baking, and the slow decrease in temperature should prevent it from cracking.)

Serve warm.

Makes 8 to 10 servings.

COCONUT PECAN TART

This decadent tart was concocted for a family New Year's Eve dinner. It's rich and satisfying — a narrow slice completes a celebration dinner.

CRUST
1 cup flour *250 mL*
½ cup brown sugar *125 mL*
1 cup butter, softened *250 mL*

Stir flour and brown sugar together in bowl. Beat in butter. Press into buttered 9 inch (23 cm) pie plate or tart pan, and bake at 325°F (160° C) for 20 minutes or until lightly golden.

TOPPING
2 eggs
1 cup brown sugar *250 mL*
1 tsp vanilla *5 mL*
2 Tbsp flour *25 mL*
½ tsp baking powder *2 mL*
dash salt
1 cup chopped pecans *250 mL*
1 cup shredded coconut *250* mL

Beat eggs and brown sugar in bowl until smooth. Beat in vanilla.

Stir together flour, baking powder and salt; stir into egg mixture, mixing well. Stir in nuts.

Spread over partially baked crust. Sprinkle with coconut, pressing into batter.

Bake at 325°F (160°C) for 20 to 25 minutes or until topping is lightly brown. (Be careful not to over-bake. Tart should be slightly syrupy.)

Serve slightly warm from the oven or at room temperature.

Makes 12 servings.

CRANBERRY MOUSSE

Diane Creber, a friend and potter, makes this dessert often, especially when serving turkey or chicken. She's often asked for the recipe, and once submitted it to a local organization for a fund-raising cookbook. "Imagine my surprise," she says, "when I saw it listed as Cranberry Moose, under the heading Game!"

2 cups fresh or frozen cranberries *500 mL*
½ cup water *125 mL*
¾ cup sugar *175 mL*
½ cup orange marmalade *125 mL*
1½ cups whipping cream *375 mL*

Combine cranberries and water in saucepan. The pectin in the cranberries acts like a gelatin, allowing the mousse to hold its shape after the mould has been removed.

Boil, reduce heat and simmer, covered for 2 minutes. Remove about 18 berries for garnish.

Cook remaining berries for 2 to 3 minutes or until soft. Press berries through sieve into bowl, discarding skins.

Stir sugar and marmalade into sieved mixture, stirring well.

Cool to room temperature. In separate bowl, beat cream until soft peaks form; fold into cranberry mixture.

Turn into buttered 5 cup (1.25 L) mould.

Cover and freeze until firm. To serve, let stand 10 minutes at room temperature.

Unmould. Dust reserved berries with sugar. Garnish mousse with sugared berries and an orange twist.

Makes 6 servings.

MAPLE MOUSSE

A neighbour on a nearby concession road runs a sugar shack in his maple bush each spring. The sap, boiled down into syrup, is nothing short of divine.

4 eggs, separated
1 cup maple syrup *250 mL*
½ tsp vanilla *2 mL*
1½ cups whipping cream *375 mL*

Beat egg yolks in heavy saucepan over low heat until light; beat in maple syrup until well blended.

Cook over low heat, stirring constantly, until mixture thickens, about 12 minutes.

Remove from heat. Stir in vanilla.

When syrup has thoroughly cooled, whip cream and fold in. Beat egg whites until stiff, and fold them in.

Pour into sherbet glasses and freeze until firm, about 3 hours.

Before serving, let stand at room temperature for a few minutes.

Makes 6 servings

▼ ▼ ▼ ▼ ▼ ▼ ▼ ▼ ▼ ▼ ▼ ▼ ▼ ▼ ▼

MAPLE SYRUP

Maple syrup is the first harvest of the new
year. When the temperature creeps up during
the day, and the sap begins to flow, but the
nights are still cool, it's sugaring season! The
sap, tapped from the tree, can simply be
drunk. But boiled down into a syrup, it is
extraordinarily sweet, and a little goes a long
way. At the beginning of the season, the syrup
is light coloured and mild flavoured, but as
the season progresses, it becomes darker and
more intense. It surpasses all other syrups as a
topping on pancakes, and although extravagant, makes a very special mousse.

▲ ▲ ▲ ▲ ▲ ▲ ▲ ▲ ▲ ▲ ▲ ▲ ▲ ▲ ▲

POVERTY CAKE

*I was not much more than a child when I met an elderly
woman whom I remember vividly. She was short, jolly
and round — the way I think of Mrs. Claus. Her house
was a weathered grey colour, without even a remnant of
peeling paint, and apple trees blossomed in her yard.
When I think now about her life, I realize how hard it
was: electricity was first connected to their barn, and only
years later to their house. She served me a slice of*
Poverty Cake *with a spoonful of applesauce and I liked
it so much that I asked her for the recipe. She told me,
"You can tell it's done when a fine field straw comes out of
the centre clean."*

1 egg
2 cups brown sugar *500 mL*
½ cup butter, softened *125 mL*
½ tsp vanilla *2 mL*
2½ cups flour *625 mL*
1 tsp baking soda *5 mL*
½ tsp nutmeg *2 mL*
½ tsp cinnamon *2 mL*
dash salt
1 cup sour milk *250 mL*
1 cup raisins *250 mL*

Beat egg in bowl. Beat in brown sugar, butter and vanilla.
Stir together flour, baking soda, nutmeg, cinnamon and salt.

If you don't have sour milk, combine 1 tbsp (15 mL) vinegar with enough milk to make 1 cup (250 mL).

Stir flour mixture into brown sugar mixture alternately with milk. Stir in raisins.

Turn into buttered 9 inch (2.5 L) cake pan and bake at 350°F (180°C) for 1 hour.

Let cool. Top with *Quick Caramel Icing*, sprinkled with chopped nuts (if desired).

Makes 1 cake.

QUICK CARAMEL ICING

*My mother, Luella Clifford, never used a candy ther-
mometer, and her icing was perfect every time. If you
don't have a candy thermometer, cook the icing until a bit
of it drizzled into cold water forms a soft ball.*

1 cup brown sugar *250 mL*
⅓ cup milk *75 mL*
2 Tbsp butter *25 mL*
pinch salt
1 Tbsp cream *15 mL*
1 tsp vanilla *5 mL*

Combine sugar, milk, butter and salt in saucepan and
cook over medium-high heat, without stirring, until mixture
reaches 234°F (112°C) on candy thermometer.

Remove from heat and cool to 110°F (45°C).

Beat until icing begins to thicken. Beat in cream and
vanilla, beating until spreading consistency.

Makes enough for a 9 inch (2.5 L) cake.

GENUINE MINCEMEAT

Jan Nightingale, who lives near Belleville, Ontario, and opened her recipe box to share this traditional winter treat, says, "Many people have no idea that mincemeat used to contain minced meat." This recipe has been handed down for five or six generations in Jan's family.

2 *lb* round steak *1 kg*
4 *lb* tart apples (about 24) *2 kg*
4 *lb* raisins *2 kg*
4 *cups* sour cherries *1 L*
2 *lb* brown sugar *1 kg*
½ *lb* mixed peel *250 g*
4 *cups* boiled apple cider *1 L*
1 *cup* suet *250 mL*
4 *tsp* ground cinnamon *20 mL*
2 *tsp* ground cloves *10 mL*
2 *tsp* ground nutmeg *10 mL*

Braise meat in water in covered skillet over medium-low heat for 25 minutes until cooked through; cool, then grind using a meat grinder or food processor.

Core, peel and chop apples.

Stir together all ingredients in large bowl, mixing well, and let sit 1 week in the refrigerator before using.

Makes enough for 12 to 15 pies.

GRANDMA'S FRUIT PUDDING

When I was a child, my grandmother would make this pudding; a generation later, my mother followed suit. It became the finalé at my holiday table, and now, my daughters have the recipe. Although the ingredient list is long, the pudding is very easy to make.

1½ cups flour *375 mL*
1 Tbsp baking powder *15 mL*
1 tsp salt *5 mL*
1 tsp cinnamon *5 mL*
½ tsp nutmeg *2 mL*
½ tsp ground ginger *2 mL*
¼ tsp ground cloves *1 mL*
1½ cups seedless raisins *375 mL*
1 cup seeded raisins, chopped *250 mL*
1 cup currants *250 mL*
¾ cup mixed peel *175 mL*
½ cup coarsely chopped almonds *125 mL*
1½ cups diced raw apple *375 mL*
1¼ cups brown sugar *300 mL*
1 cup coarse bread crumbs *250 mL*
1 cup grated carrots *250 mL*
1 cup softened butter or suet *250 mL*
3 eggs
⅓ cup cold strong coffee *75 mL*

Sift flour, baking powder, salt, and spices together three times in very large bowl.

Stir in both kinds of raisins, currants, mixed peel and almonds until well coated. Stir in apples, brown sugar, bread crumbs, carrots and softened butter.

Beat eggs and coffee in separate bowl; stir into pudding mixture, mixing well.

Turn into 12-cup (3 L) buttered mould. (I use the same pottery bowl that my grandmother once steamed her pudding in.)

Cover with two or three sheets of waxed paper, with the bottom sheet buttered, and tie with string. Place bowl in steamer or on rack in large kettle. Pour in boiling water about halfway up sides of mould or bowl.

Cover tightly and steam over low heat for 4 hours on top of stove, maintaining a gentle boil. Uncover, remove from boiling water and remove waxed paper.

Cool slightly before turning out onto serving platter. Serve hot with *Caramel Sauce* (see next page).

Makes 12 to 14 servings.

CARAMEL SAUCE

Serve with Grandma's Fruit Pudding, *or drizzled over ice cream.*

2 cups brown sugar *500 mL*
¼ cup butter *50 mL*
1¾ cups hot water *425 mL*
¼ cup cold water *50 mL*
2 Tbsp corn starch *25 mL*
1 tsp vanilla *5 mL*

Heat brown sugar and butter in saucepan over medium-high heat, stirring constantly until brown caramelized, about 5 minutes. Slowly stir in hot water. Mix cold water and corn-starch together until smooth. Stir into caramel mixture. Bring to the boil, stirring until thickened, about 8 minutes. Stir in vanilla.

Makes 2 cups (500 mL).

Mrs Morgan's Dark Christmas Cake

This wonderful recipe should be made in early November for serving at Christmas. Red and green cherries, which are traditional in Christmas cakes, have been left out because of the neon artificial colours they contain.

2 *cups* chopped dried pineapple *500 mL*
2 *cups* Lexia muscat raisins *500 mL*
3 *cups* sultana raisins *750 mL*
1½ *cups* currants 375 mL
2½ *cups* sifted flour 625 mL
1 *cup* blanched almonds *250 mL*
1 *cup* walnuts *250 mL*
1 *cup* pecans *250 mL*
1½ *cups* brandy or orange juice *375 mL*
¼ *lb* softened butter *125 g*
1½ *cups* brown sugar *375 mL*
3 eggs
1 *Tbsp* milk *15 mL*
1 *tsp* almond flavouring *5 mL*
1 *tsp* vanilla *5 mL*
½ *tsp* cinnamon *2 mL*
½ *tsp* nutmeg *2 mL*
½ *tsp* baking soda *2 mL*
½ *cup* strong coffee or orange juice *125 mL*

Mix dried fruits together in large bowl and drizzle with ½ cup (125 mL) of the brandy. Cover and let stand overnight.

Add nuts and 1 cup (250 mL) of the flour to fruit mixture. Mix well. (This keeps fruit from sinking to bottom while cake is cooking.)

Cream butter in bowl and gradually add sugar, beating until light. Beat in eggs, one at a time. Stir in milk, flavourings, spices and baking soda. Alternately stir in remaining flour and coffee, beating until smooth. Stir batter into floured fruit-nuts mixture.

Butter 3 square Christmas cake pans (varying sizes with removable bottoms) and line with heavy brown paper that has been cut and buttered. Spoon cake batter into pans, filling corners.

Place pan of boiling water on bottom of oven. Bake cakes at 275°F (140°C) in middle of oven for about 3 hours or until a straw or skewer inserted into centre of cake comes out clean.

Remove cakes from oven and cool on racks. When cool, carefully remove brown paper.

Wrap cakes first in waxed paper and then in tin foil and store in tins. Every 2 weeks, unwrap, drizzle with remaining brandy and re-wrap.

Makes 3 cakes.

CHOCOLATE SPECIALS

*This no-bake recipe is quick to make and never fails. It is
a favourite for winter holiday celebrations and
summer picnics alike.*

3 cups rolled oats *750 mL*
6 Tbsp unsweetened cocoa powder, sifted *90 mL*
1 cup unsweetened shredded coconut *250 mL*
2 cups sugar *500 mL*
½ cup milk *125 mL*
½ cup butter *125 mL*
1 tsp vanilla *5 mL*

Stir together oats, cocoa and coconut in bowl and set
aside. Bring sugar, milk and butter to boil in saucepan; pour
over oats and mix well.

Stir in vanilla. Drop by teaspoonfuls onto waxed-paper-
lined baking sheet.

When cool, store in covered container at room temperature. Best eaten within 3 days.

Makes 36 cookies.

▼ ▼ ▼ ▼ ▼ ▼ ▼ ▼ ▼ ▼ ▼ ▼ ▼ ▼ ▼ ▼

WINTER BAKING

From the early harvest of maple syrup and
asparagus in the spring to late-ripening apples
and parsnips (which need frosty nights to
sweeten) in the fall, country cooks tend to
serve the foods that grow around them. But
in the winter, when locally grown fresh fruits
and vegetables are no longer available, we frequently turn to dried ingredients and exotic
imports, such as coconut. Coconut is dense
and rich; two tablespoons has about 50
calories. It does, however, sweeten desserts,
and it brings tropical dreams close.

▲ ▲ ▲ ▲ ▲ ▲ ▲ ▲ ▲ ▲ ▲ ▲ ▲ ▲ ▲ ▲

CAROB BALLS

Even small children can help make these healthful
morsels, which are quick to mix and require no baking.

1½ cups peanut butter *375 mL*
1 cup honey *250 mL*
1½ cups quick-cooking rolled oats *375 mL*
¾ cup carob powder *175 mL*
2 Tbsp sunflower oil *25 mL*
½ tsp vanilla *2 mL*
sesame seeds or coconut

Mix together peanut butter and honey in bowl; stir in rolled oats, carob powder, oil and vanilla.

Butter the palms of your hands and roll mixture into balls.

Roll balls in sesame seeds or shredded coconut.

Cover with plastic wrap and store in refrigerator for up to a week.

Makes 30 balls.

▼ ▼ ▼ ▼ ▼ ▼ ▼ ▼ ▼ ▼ ▼ ▼ ▼ ▼ ▼

CAROB

Carob is often used as a substitute for chocolate, particularly by those allergic to chocolate. It comes from tamarind pods, which
grow in the Mediterranean region, and are
dried and ground into carob flour. For those
lucky enough to find fresh tamarind, the
spicy, date-apricot flavoured pulp can be
eaten raw. Ground carob is quite readily
found in groceries and health food stores. It
can be combined with flour (¾ cup flour and
¼ cup carob can replace 1 cup of flour in a
recipe), but beware, because it scorches easily
— bake at 300°F or less.

▲ ▲ ▲ ▲ ▲ ▲ ▲ ▲ ▲ ▲ ▲ ▲ ▲ ▲ ▲

HOT FUDGE PUDDING

This self-saucing pudding couldn't be simpler or faster to prepare. It has been a favourite among our children, who pleaded for it instead of birthday cake when they were younger. It's a satisfying dish to serve in winter when fresh fruits and vegetables are not as readily available or inexpensive as they are in season.

1 cup flour *250 mL*
¾ cup white sugar *175 mL*
6 Tbsp unsweetened cocoa powder *90 mL*
2 tsp baking powder *10 mL*
½ tsp salt *2 mL*
½ cup milk *125 mL*
2 Tbsp oil *25 mL*
1 tsp vanilla *5 mL*
¾ cup brown sugar *175 mL*
1 ¾ cups hot water *400 mL*

Sift together flour, white sugar, 2 Tbsp (25 mL) of the cocoa, baking powder and salt in a bowl. In another bowl, beat milk, oil and vanilla; stir into dry ingredients. Pour into greased 8 inch (2 L) square pan. Stir together brown sugar, remaining 4 Tbsp (60 mL) cocoa and hot water; pour over batter. Bake at 350°F (180°C) for 45 minutes.

Makes 8 servings.

▼ ▼ ▼ ▼ ▼ ▼ ▼ ▼ ▼ ▼ ▼ ▼ ▼ ▼ ▼ ▼

COCOA MEANT CASH

In Aztec lore, Quetzalcoatl, a feathered serpent and the gardener of paradise, taught the people how to grow the cacao tree and harvest its beans. When the Spaniards arrived in the New World, the Aztecs were paying taxes in cocoa beans and making a chocolate drink from the beans.

Cocoa and chocolate are both products of the cacao tree; they have simply undergone different processes. Throughout the ages they've been called aphrodisiacs, cures for fevers, tonics to prolong life and a quick source of energy. However, one of the best reasons for eating chocolate and cocoa is the taste.

▲ ▲ ▲ ▲ ▲ ▲ ▲ ▲ ▲ ▲ ▲ ▲ ▲ ▲ ▲ ▲

PEANUT BUTTER OATMEAL COOKIES

Peanut butter cookies may not seem to be celebration fare, and yet these cookies celebrate childhood. Make them with your kids, then enjoy a treat as healthful and nutritious as a cookie can be.

1 cup flour *250 mL*
1½ tsp baking powder *7 mL*
½ tsp salt *2 mL*
¼ tsp baking soda *1 mL*
⅔ cup soft butter *150 mL*
1 cup smooth peanut butter *250 mL*
1 cup brown sugar *250 mL*
⅓ cup white sugar *75 mL*
1 tsp vanilla *5 mL*
2 eggs
1 cup quick-cooking rolled oats *250 mL*

Combine flour, baking powder, salt and soda in bowl.

Beat butter in another large bowl until creamy; beat in peanut butter and continue beating until blended. Gradually beat in brown and white sugar and vanilla. Beat in eggs, beating well. Finally, stir in rolled oats and flour mixture.

Drop dough by level spoonfuls well apart on greased

cookie sheets. Flatten with fork. Bake at 350°F (180°C) for 8 to 10 minutes or until lightly browned.

Makes 36 cookies.

▼ ▼ ▼ ▼ ▼ ▼ ▼ ▼ ▼ ▼ ▼ ▼ ▼ ▼ ▼ ▼

PEANUT BUTTER

Peanuts are native to the tropical regions of the Americas. They have found their way around the world, where they may be known as groundnuts or groundpeas. Peanuts provide oil and vitamins, and when eaten with cooked whole grains, are a good source of protein.

▲ ▲ ▲ ▲ ▲ ▲ ▲ ▲ ▲ ▲ ▲ ▲ ▲ ▲ ▲ ▲

▼ ▼ ▼ ▼ ▼ ▼ ▼ ▼ ▼ ▼ ▼ ▼ ▼ ▼ ▼ ▼

OATS

Oats — along with wheat, barley, millet and other whole grains — contain vitamins, minerals, starches and proteins, as well as vitamin B6. They are also high in fibre, important in reducing cholesterol levels and in preventing cancer and other diseases. Separated oat grains that have been flattened, rather than ground into flour or meal, are called simply rolled oats. Rolled oats have a delicious nutty flavour, adding both taste and texture to recipes. Substituting up to one-third the total wheat flour in cookie, bread and muffin recipes with rolled oats. For every one cup of flour being substituted, use one and one-third cups rolled oats.

▲ ▲ ▲ ▲ ▲ ▲ ▲ ▲ ▲ ▲ ▲ ▲ ▲ ▲ ▲ ▲

COUNTRY FAVOURITE NUTS & BOLTS

Mid-December is the ideal time to prepare this treat, which is perfect for long winter evenings. Over the years, making Nuts & Bolts *has become a pre-Christmas ritual. Often we made it on the same day that the tree was decorated; then, we would sit at the end of the day exclaiming how this was the most beautiful tree ever and these the best treats. Now our children make it for their children, and we tuck it into pretty tins and jars to give to friends and neighbours during the holiday season.*

1 box square, wheat cereal *675 g*
1 box doughnut-shaped oat cereal *300 g*
½ lb mixed nuts *250 g*
½ lb cashews *250 g*
1 lb skinless peanuts *500 g*
¾ lb small pretzels *375 g*
2 cups vegetable oil *500 mL*
3 Tbsp Worcestershire sauce *45 mL*
1 Tbsp garlic powder *15 mL*
1 Tbsp seasoned salt *15 mL*
½ Tbsp salt *7 mL*
1 tsp paprika *5 mL*
½ tsp cayenne *2 mL*
½ tsp Tabasco sauce *2 mL*

Pour equal amounts of cereal into large roasting pan until about three-quarters full (you'll need nearly one large box of each cereal).

Stir in nuts and pretzels.

Whisk together oil, Worcestershire sauce, garlic powder, seasoned salt, salt, paprika, cayenne and Tabasco sauce in bowl.

Stir into cereal-nut mixture, mixing well.

Bake at 250°F (120°C) for 2 hours, stirring every 15 minutes. Store in covered jars for up to 6 weeks.

Makes about 40 cups (10 L).

CARAMEL CORN

Without a doubt, this is the best caramel corn possible. If you believe that celebrations warrant a little extravagance, indulge. It's a scrumptious treat to take to parties and best eaten the same day as made.

1 cup popping corn *250 mL*
2 cups brown sugar *500 mL*
1 cup butter *250 mL*
½ cup light corn syrup *125 mL*
1 tsp salt *5 mL*
1 tsp vanilla *5 mL*
½ tsp baking soda *2 mL*
peanuts (optional)

Pop corn and set aside.

Heat sugar, butter, corn syrup and salt in saucepan and boil for 5 minutes. Remove from heat and stir in vanilla and baking soda.

Stir together popped corn, hot syrup and as many peanuts as desired (if using) in large roasting pan.

Bake at 250°F (120°C) for 1 hour, stirring every 15 minutes.

Makes about 16 cups.

Healthy Canada

Health and Welfare Canada   Santé et Bien-être social Canada

CANADA'S
Food Guide
TO HEALTHY EATING

Enjoy a variety of foods from each group every day.

Choose lower-fat foods more often.

Grain Products
Choose whole grain and enriched products more often.

Vegetables & Fruit
Choose dark green and orange vegetables and orange fruit more often.

Milk Products
Choose lower-fat milk products more often.

Meat & Alternatives
Choose leaner meats, poultry and fish, as well as dried peas, beans and lentils more often.

Canada

Ministry of Health
Ontario

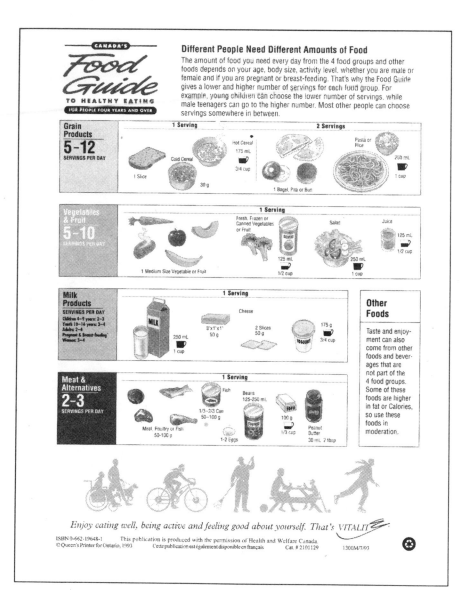

Canada's Food Guide to Healthy Eating
FOR PEOPLE FOUR YEARS AND OVER

Different People Need Different Amounts of Food

The amount of food you need every day from the 4 food groups and other foods depends on your age, body size, activity level, whether you are male or female and if you are pregnant or breast-feeding. That's why the Food Guide gives a lower and higher number of servings for each food group. For example, young children can choose the lower number of servings, while male teenagers can go to the higher number. Most other people can choose servings somewhere in between.

Grain Products
5-12 SERVINGS PER DAY

1 Serving — 1 Slice · Cold Cereal · Hot Cereal 175 mL 3/4 cup · 30 g
2 Servings — 1 Bagel, Pita or Bun · Pasta or Rice 250 mL 1 cup

Vegetables & Fruit
5-10 SERVINGS PER DAY

1 Serving — 1 Medium Size Vegetable or Fruit · Fresh, Frozen or Canned Vegetables or Fruit 125 mL 1/2 cup · Salad 250 mL 1 cup · Juice 125 mL 1/2 cup

Milk Products
SERVINGS PER DAY
Children 4–9 years: 2–3
Youth 10–16 years: 3–4
Adults: 2–4
Pregnant & Breast-feeding Women: 3–4

1 Serving — Milk 250 mL 1 cup · Cheese 3"x1"x1" 50 g · 2 Slices 50 g · 175 g 3/4 cup

Meat & Alternatives
2-3 SERVINGS PER DAY

1 Serving — Meat, Poultry or Fish 50-100 g · Fish 1/3-2/3 Can 50-100 g · 1-2 Eggs · Beans 125-250 mL · Tofu 100 g 1/3 cup · Peanut Butter 30 mL, 2 tbsp

Other Foods

Taste and enjoyment can also come from other foods and beverages that are not part of the 4 food groups. Some of these foods are higher in fat or Calories, so use these foods in moderation.

Enjoy eating well, being active and feeling good about yourself. That's VITALITY

ISBN 0-662-19648-1   This publication is produced with the permission of Health and Welfare Canada.
© Queen's Printer for Ontario, 1993   Cette publication est également disponible en français   Cat. # 2101129   1300M/7/93

INDEX

OTHER BOOKS FROM SECOND STORY PRESS